50 AMAZING THINGS KIDS NEED TO KNOW ABOUT MATHEMATICS

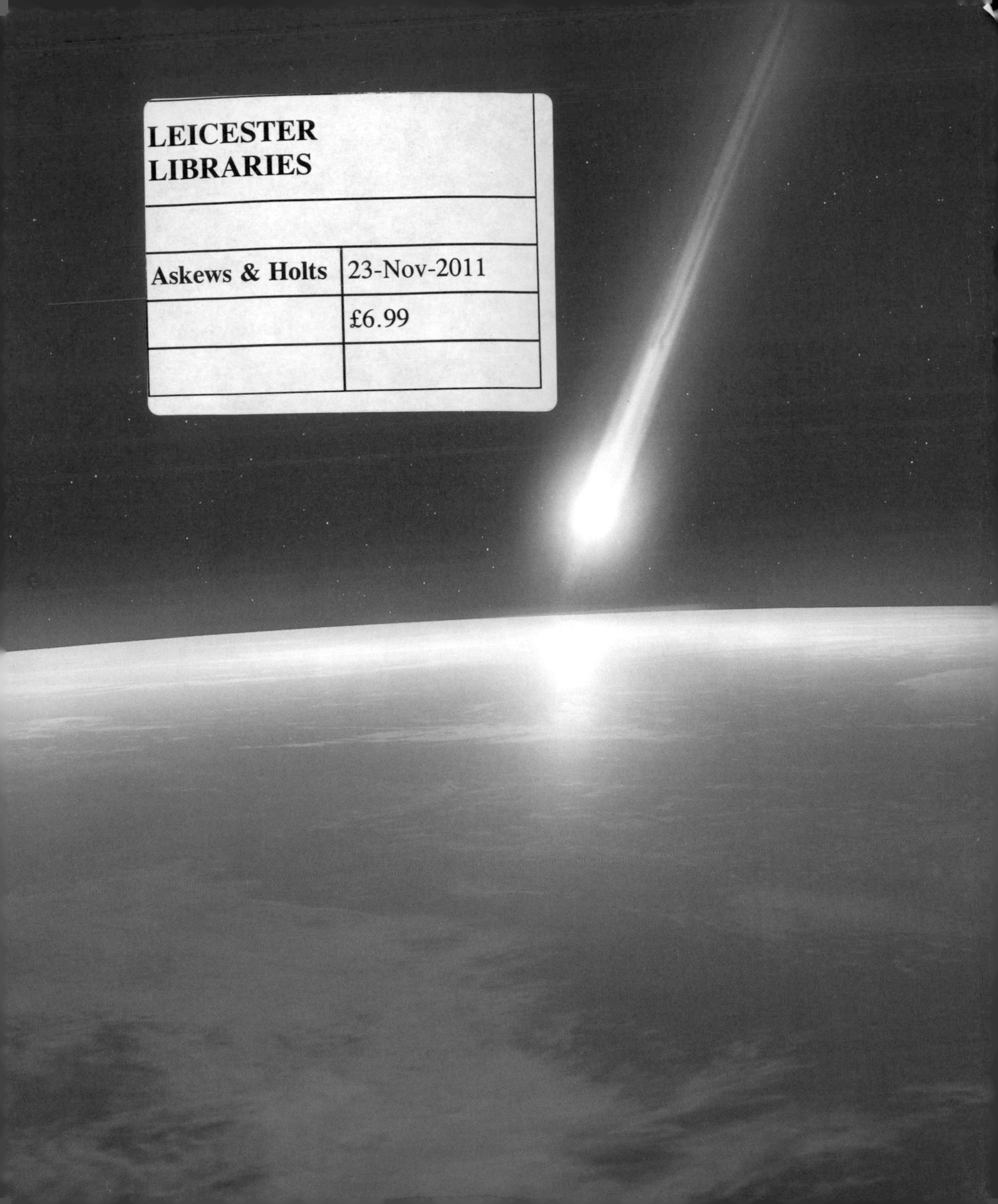

50 AMAZING THINGS KIDS NEED TO KNOW ABOUT MATHEMATICS

ANNE ROONEY

Quercus

CONTENTS

INTRODUCTION

Have you ever looked up at the stars and wondered if they go on for ever? Or whether someone out there is looking at a sky that has us in it? Perhaps you have wondered how GPS knows exactly where you are. Mathematics can answer all of these questions and many more!

This book helps you to see the mathematics behind everyday situations and behind some more bizarre events, too. How would an octopus or a robot count? Could you read the numbers carved into a Roman pillar, or work out which day of the week it was if you were whizzed backwards in time? More usefully, mathematics can help you increase your chances of winning in a game, make a scale model of something huge (or tiny), and see around corners.

You might think that mathematics is just numbers and symbols,

but it is actually very practical. Without it, we could not make buildings and bridges that stay up, send spacecraft into orbit, build computers or work out what the weather will be like.

There aren't many people who work only as mathematicians, but many jobs need a good understanding of mathematics. Scientists use mathematics as they make discoveries and explain the world around us. Mathematics can also help artists to paint beautiful pictures and musicians to write

This book will show you some of the magic of mathematics. You can read it from cover to cover, or dip in and out as there are lots of different topics to discover. Once you have started, though, you will probably find you are drawn in and will want to learn more and more. There are puzzles and tricks to try, things to work out and suggestions of how to use mathematics in the real world.

There is a fascinating world of numbers out there waiting to be explored. You will find amazing things to do with numbers – such as count more things than could possibly exist or think of a number so long it could never be written down. Mathematics really can blow your mind!

memorable music. It is not just about patterns we impose on the world, but also about patterns we discover in nature. Did you know that the arrangement of seeds in a sunflower, the branching pattern of blood vessels and the shape of a snail's shell are all mathematically linked? Or that the distance between the source of a river and the sea is related to the equation that lets us work out the area of a circle? Mathematics is everywhere – and it's mind-boggling!

1 HOW TO BE A POP STAR

Mathematics and music may seem miles apart, but they are, in fact, closely connected. If you want to be a great musician, it helps if you can understand the mathematics behind music. Many great mathematicians, including Einstein, were also musicians.

MUSICAL NOTES

A note is a single musical sound. When someone plays a musical instrument, the notes create sound waves in the air. The pitch of the note – how high or low it is – depends on the frequency of the sound wave (see box on page 9).

Notes are arranged in octaves. An octave has eight notes, called A, B, C, D, E, F, G. After G, the next octave starts again at A. All notes with the same letter sound similar – they are just at a different pitch.

WAVY MUSIC

Music is made up of sound waves – vibrations that travel through the air to your ear. The wavelength of a sound wave is the distance between one peak (or trough) and the next. The frequency of a sound is the number of waves per second, and is measured in hertz (Hz). A high-frequency sound makes a high-pitched note, and it has more waves per second than a low-frequency sound, which makes a low-pitched note. For example, the A above middle C has a frequency of 440 Hz

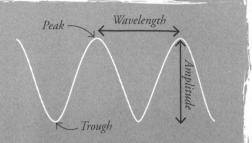

(440 waves per second). The amplitude is the height of the sound wave. The greater the amplitude, the louder the sound.

☞ When you pluck or strum the strings of a guitar, the vibrations from the strings make sound waves.

The pitch of a note changes as the frequency of the sound wave increases or decreases. The sound wave's frequency doubles each time you move up an octave. For example, the frequency of middle A is 440 Hz, and the next A up has a frequency of 880 Hz. If you go down an octave, A has a frequency of 220 Hz – half of 440 Hz.

HALF-NOTES

There are also half-notes, or semitones, that sit between the eight notes in an octave. You might expect that, with eight whole notes, there would be 16 semitones in an octave – but there are just 12 half-notes. This is where the mathematics becomes important.

To move up one half-note in pitch, you need to multiply the frequency of the starting note by 1.0594... (the digits after the decimal point go on and on). This is not just any number – when you multiply 1.0594... by itself 12 times, the answer is 2, which is why the frequency of a note doubles after 12 semitones.

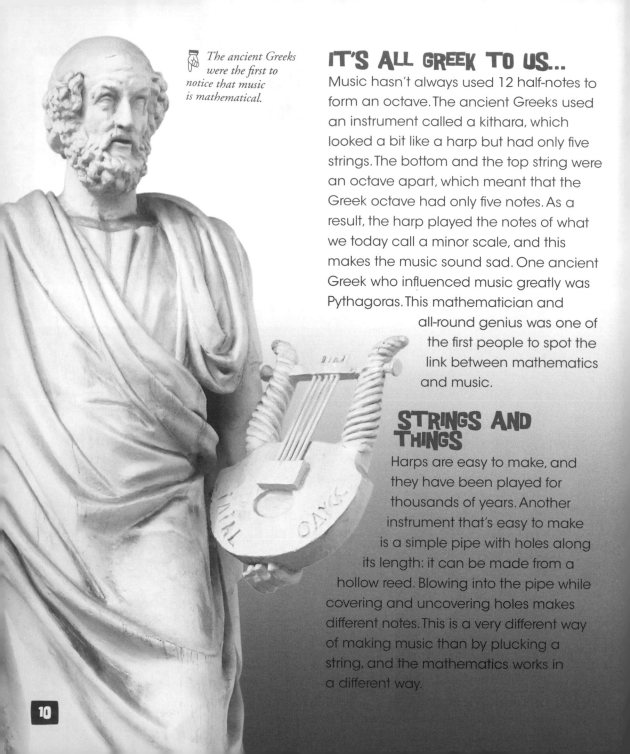

The ancient Greeks were the first to notice that music is mathematical.

IT'S ALL GREEK TO US...

Music hasn't always used 12 half-notes to form an octave. The ancient Greeks used an instrument called a kithara, which looked a bit like a harp but had only five strings. The bottom and the top string were an octave apart, which meant that the Greek octave had only five notes. As a result, the harp played the notes of what we today call a minor scale, and this makes the music sound sad. One ancient Greek who influenced music greatly was Pythagoras. This mathematician and all-round genius was one of the first people to spot the link between mathematics and music.

STRINGS AND THINGS

Harps are easy to make, and they have been played for thousands of years. Another instrument that's easy to make is a simple pipe with holes along its length: it can be made from a hollow reed. Blowing into the pipe while covering and uncovering holes makes different notes. This is a very different way of making music than by plucking a string, and the mathematics works in a different way.

Harmonics and harmonies

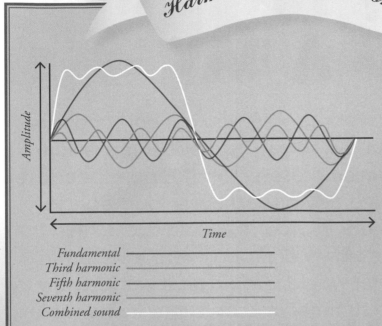

Amplitude

Time

Fundamental ——————————
Third harmonic ——————————
Fifth harmonic ——————————
Seventh harmonic ——————————
Combined sound ——————————

The lowest frequency at which a string vibrates is the fundamental frequency. All the other harmonics have frequencies that are multiples of this frequency. For example, the third harmonic (the grey wave) has a frequency that is three times as much, and a wavelength that's one-third of the fundamental. When the notes in a harmonic have waves that fit together, as the waves on the left do, the combined sound is satisfying. When the waves don't fit inside one another, the sound is disturbing or sad.

When you play a flute, the note produced is pure – if the note is a middle A, that is all you will hear, with no other sound. But if you pluck a string on a guitar, harp or violin to produce an A, the string 'twangs' – you can hear other sounds behind or around the A note of the string. This effect is called 'harmonics'. These extra sounds have frequencies that are exact multiples of the base note (the note you were playing) – so the wave may be a half or a third of the base note, for example (see the box above). Harmonics of A include C# (C sharp) and E; the notes A, C# and E make up the chord of A major, which sounds happy and satisfying. See? Mathematics is behind music!

see for yourself

Try making your own guitar by stretching rubber bands across a shoe box. You can tune the rubber bands to play the right notes by making them tighter or looser.

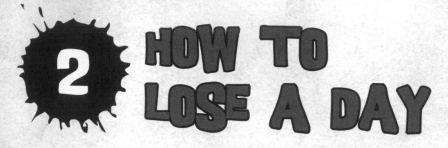

2 HOW TO LOSE A DAY

If your birthday is on February 29, you get only one true birthday every four years, so you had better make sure you ask for an extra-nice present! This happens because February 29 is an extra day added every four years to help keep the calendar in order. If we did not do this, the calendar would slowly drift and eventually summer and winter would swap over. It would snow in the summer and be sunny in the winter.

WHAT MAKES A YEAR?

A year is the length of time it takes Earth to go around the Sun, which is about 365 days. Unfortunately, it is not exactly 365 days: it is 365.242374 days. This looks near enough to 365.25 days for there to be an easy fix, and Julius Caesar introduced one in 45 BC – the leap year. Every fourth year, an extra day is added to the year. This extra day is now put at the end of February.

We could have had a January 32 or even April 31 instead, but it is fairer to give the extra leap day to February, as it has only 28 days normally.

DRIFTING YEARS

The extra day still doesn't stop the years drifting very slowly, however. At the end of a century, when the year ends in '00' (for example, 1800 or 1900) we skip the leap year. So if a person was born on February 29, 1896, he or she would not have a true birthday for eight years!

And we are still not quite there... When the century can be divided by 400, we keep the leap year – like the year 2000. Even with this system, the calendar will still lose a day every 8,000 years. There is a suggestion that the year 4000 should skip its leap day, but there is no urgent need to decide that yet as it's quite a long way off!

A person born on 29 February is called a 'leapling'.

DIFFERENT CALENDARS

The calendar introduced by Julius Caesar in 45 BC was called the Julian calendar. But there was a difference of about 11 minutes between a real year and a year according to this calendar. Over time, this led to problems. The calendar drifted by a day every 131 years. In 1582, Pope Gregory XIII introduced a new calendar, called the Gregorian calendar, and skipped ten days to put everything back where it should be.

In Britain, it was 1752 before the calendar changed – by which time it was out by another day. People went to bed on September 2, 1752, and when they woke up it was September 14!

The Maya people of South America have used a calendar to record their history since the 5th century BC. Today, their calendar is still used by some people in Guatemala. In the Mayan calendar, each date is represented by two numbers. The first number is from a set of symbols that are linked with mythology, and the other is taken from a 13-day cycle. Apart from representing each day with two numbers, the calendar is different from others because it has a start date and an end date. It started in 3115 BC and will end in 2012. Those who still use the calendar believe that the end of the world will coincide with the end of the calendar!

see for yourself

On Yasmin's sixth birthday, she had lived 2,191 days. On his sixth birthday, Edgar had lived 2,192 days. How is this possible?

Answer: They were born in different years: Yasmin's six years include one leap year (for example, 2001–2007; leap year in 2004) and Edgar's include two leap years (for example, 2003–2009; leap years in 2004 and 2008).

LEAP SECONDS

To even things out, we have leap seconds every now and then. These are extra seconds snuck into the clock in the middle of the night when they won't have too much impact on people. They can be added at the end of June or December and are announced about six months in advance. The time reported for that extra second is 23:59:60.

AND HOW TO GAIN TIME...

We make a lot of effort to keep our clocks in order, but time does not always pass at the same rate. Scientist, mathematician and genius Albert Einstein showed that time passes more slowly if you travel very quickly – at more than 30,000 km (18,750 miles) per second – or if you are very far from a body with a gravitational field (such as a planet). This has been tested at lower speeds, where the effect is not so great. Using a really fast aircraft, the experiment proved Einstein was right. If we could put a clock in just the right place so that the gravitational fields of the Sun and the planets were balanced, it would be 0.49 seconds per year faster than a clock on Earth's surface.

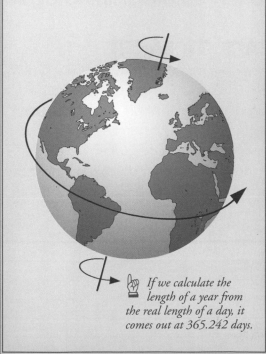

Days, weeks and months

A day is 24 hours long – or is it? For all practical purposes it is, but the time Earth takes to rotate once on its axis is actually 23 hours, 56 minutes and 4.091 seconds. It would be quite inconvenient to have days of that length, though.

To complicate things even more, Earth's rotation is slowing down ever so slightly, so a day is gradually becoming even shorter. But don't worry – it won't stop rotating any time soon: the Sun will have frazzled up Earth before that happens.

If we calculate the length of a year from the real length of a day, it comes out at 365.242 days.

3 HOW TO THINK LIKE A ROBOT

How do you like to count? 1, 2, 3, 4, 5, 6, 7, 8, 9, 10… We have nine different symbols for the digits we use – ten if you count zero (0) – yet we can write numbers of unlimited size with them. Why ten? Probably because we have ten fingers and thumbs, which makes counting to ten before starting again the easiest thing to do.

BACK TO BASES

When we count, we usually use a system called base-10, which means that we count up to nine, then start reusing the digits with '10'. This number is made up of one ten and no ones. When we get to '99' (nine tens and nine ones), we then move on to '100', which stands for one hundred (10 x 10) and no tens or ones.

But you can count using any other number as the basis, or 'base', for the system. For example, if we counted in base-5, the numbers would go: 0, 1, 2, 3, 4, 10… Here '10' means one five and no ones. However, the third column of numbers in base-5 stands for the number of 25s (5 x 5). So '100' in base-5 stands for one 25 and no other units.

Base-10			
hundreds	tens	ones	
		1	one
	1	0	ten
	1	1	eleven
1	0	0	one hundred

Base-5			
twenty-fives	fives	ones	
		1	one
	1	0	five
	1	1	six
1	0	0	twenty five

Most cartoon characters have only three fingers and a thumb on each hand – perhaps they should count in base-8!

ROBOTS' FINGERS

We could build a robot with any number of fingers, but it would not need to use them to count as it has a computer as a brain. Computers count in base-2, or binary. This has only two numbers: 0 and 1. The number '10' means one two and nothing extra. As you can see from the table below, numbers in base-2 get very long very quickly.

Base-2			
fours	twos	ones	
		1	one
	1	0	two
	1	1	three
1	0	0	four

Computers use binary because data can be stored using a simple on/off switch, with '1' for 'on' and '0'' for 'off'. Numbers can be coded as magnetic charges – either there is a charge or there is not – and this is how hard disks store data.

MORE THAN TEN

Robots and computers actually have more than one way of counting. For higher-level functions, they use a system called hexadecimal. This is base-16: it doesn't start reusing digits until it gets to 16. As we do not have 15 different number symbols, hexadecimal uses the letters A–F as extra numbers:

0, 1, 2, 3, 4, 5, 6, 7, 8, 9, A, B, C, D, E, F

The number '10' means '16', and the number '100' means '256' (16 x 16).

Base-10 (Decimal)	16	256	4096	65,536
Base-16 (Hexadecimal)	10	100	1,000	10,000

Here are some more interesting numbers using the letter symbols in base-16:

Base-10	18	29	32	100	731	1000
Base-16	12	1D	20	64	2DB	3E8

COUNTING IN OCTOPUS

If octopuses had become the dominant species on Earth, counting might have been in base-8 (called octal):

0, 1, 2, 3, 4, 5, 6, 7, 10, 11...

And if the dinosaurs had not had such a nasty episode with an asteroid, Tyrannosaurus (with three claws on each hand) counting in base-6 might now be the order of the day.

It would not make any difference to the rules of mathematics – they will work in any base system. The relationship between the sides of a triangle, or of the circumference of a circle to its radius, is exactly the same if we count in binary, base-3, octal, decimal or hexadecimal.

If we ever meet aliens, their spacecraft will work using the same mathematical principles as ours, even if they have four arms, 23 fingers and count in base-23.

see for yourself

How would you write your age if you were a robot (binary)? Or a Tyrannosaurus (base-6)? Or an octopus (octal)? If you were a robot, when could you celebrate your 1,000,000th birthday?

Answer:
1,000,000 in base-2 is 64 in base-10, so it would be your 64th birthday.

Have you ever wondered why we have 60 seconds in a minute and 60 minutes in an hour? We inherited this system from the people of ancient Babylon. Around 4,000 years ago, they used a number system that relied on base-60. Luckily, they did not have to remember 59 different digits. They used two symbols, which they repeated and grouped, one symbol meaning '1' and the other meaning '10'. Sixty is a very useful number to use as it can be divided by many numbers: 2, 3, 4, 5, 6, 10, 12, 15, 20, 30. Ten is not as good, as it can be divided only by two and five.

The Babylonians divided the day into 24 hours. The division of a circle into 360° (6 x 60) also began with the Babylonians.

☞ *With eight tentacles, an octopus might be great at counting to eight.*

Base-10 (Decimal)	0	1	2	3	4	5	6	7	8	9	10	11	12	13	14	15
Base-2 (Binary)	0	1	10	11	100	101	110	111	1000	1001	1010	1011	1100	1101	1110	1111
Base-8 (Octal)	0	1	2	3	4	5	6	7	10	11	12	13	14	15	16	17
Base-16 (Hexadecimal)	0	1	2	3	4	5	6	7	8	9	A	B	C	D	E	F

HOW TO MAKE A MAGIC SQUARE

4

People have been fascinated by number patterns throughout history. Magic squares were invented more than 4,000 years ago, and since then they have been used to predict the future, ward off disease, and ensure long life – but they haven't always been effective.

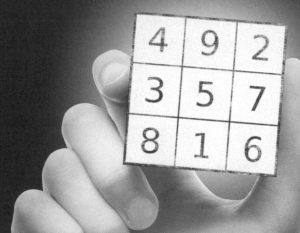

THAT'S MAGIC!

A magic square is a grid with a different number in each cell, chosen so that all the rows, columns and diagonals add up to the same total.

A magic square with sides of three cells is called an order-3 square and has nine squares. It generally uses the numbers 1 to 9; an order-4 square uses the numbers 1 to 16, and so on.

The more cells you add to the grid, the harder it becomes to make a magic square – but the number of possible magic squares increases rapidly. There is no magic square for an order-2 square,

LO SHU AND THE MAGIC TURTLE

A legend from China tells of a terrible flood of the River Lo more than 2,500 years ago. King Yu was trying to channel the water out to sea, when a turtle came out of the water with a strange pattern of dots on its shell, arranged in a 3-by-3 grid. The sum of the numbers shown in each of the rows, columns and diagonals came to 15, which is the number of days in each of the 24 months of the Chinese calendar. The people living near the River Lo started to use the magic square, called Lo Shu, as a symbol of balance to control the forces of the river.

but there are 880 possible order-3 magic squares and 275,305,224 order-4 magic squares. For an order-5 magic square there are thought to be 1.7745×10^{19} solutions – that's 17,745 followed by 15 zeroes!

WORKING IT OUT

Use the squares on the right to help you to see how magic squares work. Start by writing 1 in the middle of the top row. Now make successive moves, to the right and up, wrapping around to the bottom or left of the square to add the remaining numbers. If a square is already filled, move down one instead.

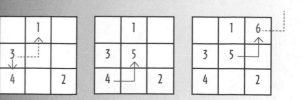

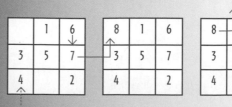

5 HOW TO MAKE A MILLION RABBITS

Have you ever looked at a sunflower and noticed that the seeds are arranged in a spiral? It is a very special spiral – and once you start looking for it, it crops up all over the place. It all started with rabbits...

FIBONACCI'S RABBITS

In 1202, the Italian mathematician Leonardo Pisano (nicknamed 'Fibonacci') wondered what would happen if he put two rabbits in a field and waited long enough for them to have babies. These rabbits would then have babies and so on, until you had a field full of rabbits. Fibonacci worked out how many rabbits there would be, assuming no foxes got into the field. He started with a pair of imaginary rabbits (1).

They were too young to breed, so there was still only a pair after a month. The next month, the rabbits had two babies, so there were two pairs (2). The next month, the original pair had two more babies, but the new rabbits were too young to have babies, so there were three pairs (3). By the next month, the first set of babies were old enough to breed – and the original couple had two more babies – so there were five pairs (5). And so it goes on.

NUMBER SEQUENCE

Pisano did not know a lot about rabbits or he would have realized that they do not breed quite like that. But he came up with a series of numbers from his imagined perfect rabbit breeding. This series is called the Fibonacci sequence.

MAGIC RABBIT NUMBERS

Fibonacci's sequence is written like this:

1, 1, 2, 3, 5, 8, 13, 21, 34, 55, 89, 144, and so on.

To find the next number in the sequence, add together the two previous numbers:
$1 + 1 = 2, 1 + 2 = 3, 2 + 3 = 5$, and so on.

So the next number after 144 is:
$89 + 144 = 233$
And the next number after that is:
$144 + 233 = 377$

Fibonacci's sequence tells us the number of pairs of rabbits that you might end up with if you started off with one pair.

Most plants grow leaves all around the stem. As we look up the stem, the leaves come out of it at different places, generally following a spiral pattern. If you think of the bottom leaf as 0, and count leaves until you come to one directly above leaf 0, it will generally be a Fibonacci number. And if you count the spirals in between, there is generally a Fibonacci number of spirals, too. Fibonacci numbers can be seen in all sorts of plants. For example, the sections in fruit and vegetables are usually Fibonacci numbers – bananas have three sections, while apples have five.

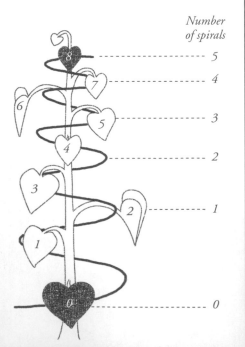

Number of spirals

PINEAPPLES AND PINE CONES

The knobbles on pine cones and pineapples are arranged in spirals. A pine cone has eight spirals going clockwise and 13 going anticlockwise – 8 and 13 are consecutive Fibonacci numbers.

☞ *The number of clockwise and anticlockwise spirals on a sunflower follow Fibonacci's series.*

A pineapple has three sets of spirals formed by its hexagonal knobbles. Five shallow spirals go to the right; eight steeper spirals go to the left; and 13 very steep spirals go to the right. And, of course, 5, 8 and 13 are consecutive Fibonacci numbers.

PETALS, SEEDS AND FIBONACCI

Have you ever counted the number of petals on a flower? If you have, you'll have noticed that a lily usually has three petals, buttercups have five and a daisy often has 34 or 55 petals. As you now know, these are all Fibonacci numbers! But it's not just the number of petals on a flower that has a Fibonacci connection. On a sunflower, the seeds in the middle are in consecutive Fibonacci numbers, such as 21 and 34 or 55 and 34, of clockwise and anticlockwise spirals.

see for yourself

When you go outside in the winter, look at the bare trees. Tree growth follows a Fibonacci pattern, with branches regularly splitting into two, then splitting again.

6 HOW TO COUNT TO INFINITY

Infinity is bigger than the biggest number you can imagine – and then some. Or smaller than the smallest number you can imagine. Numbers go on and on for ever in both directions, but it's more complicated than it sounds.

UNENDING BIGNESS

Start counting – how far can you get? If you counted all day, at perhaps two numbers a second, you could get to 115,200 in 16 hours, without pausing to eat or talk. If you did that all year, taking off only your birthday, you could get to 41,932,800. If you did it every year from age 5 to age 90, you would get to 3,564,288,000 – just over three-and-a-half billion. Now imagine some creature started at the beginning of the Universe and kept counting at the same rate until now: it would have got to 49,008,960,000,000,000,000,000. That is still nowhere near infinity. We can write a bigger number than that just by adding '1' to the end. And that is how it always will be – however much you count, you can always count more. You can never run out of numbers.

Nothing can be bigger than the Universe – but is the Universe infinite? If it is, it goes on for ever and ever. If it is finite, you might be able to get to the edge of it, or back to where you started from if you could travel far enough.

Scientists believe the Universe started with a Big Bang. Everything was created in a gigantic explosion that made time, space and matter – and then it all expanded very rapidly and carried on expanding. Now, if it can get bigger still, we could say that it is not infinite because infinity is the end of bigness. Or we could say it is infinite as there is nothing outside the Universe, and infinity gets bigger as the Universe grows.

Is the Universe infinite? We don't know if it has an end or if it goes on for ever.

AN INFINITY OF INFINITIES

There is a funny thing about infinity – even though nothing can be bigger, there is more than one infinity. As positive numbers keep going for ever, so do negative numbers, in the other direction – so there's a negative infinity, too. And both odd and even numbers go on for ever. The infinity of all numbers is obviously twice the size of the infinity of odd or even numbers, but that doesn't make sense. Once you get that far, there's no stopping – there's an infinity of multiples of three, and of five; then there's an infinity of decimal numbers between 0 and 1, and between every other pair of numbers – in fact, there's an infinity of infinities.

HOW TO BE A GENIUS

Do you ever struggle to get your head around the numbers in class? Or can you whizz through questions in no time and sit drawing cartoons while everyone else finishes? What if the question was 'Find the square root of 758,396,521'? Some people can do hard sums like that almost instantly!

50 49 48 47 46 45 44 43 42 41 40 39 38 37 36 35 34 33 32 31 30 29 28 27 26 25

51 52 53 54 55 56 57 58 59 60 61 62 63 64 65 66 67 68 69 70 71 72 73 74 75 76

Savants are people who have astonishing ability in a particular field. Mathematical savants instantly know answers that everyone else struggles to work out. They can give the solution to difficult calculations, remember long strings of numbers and give square roots without a calculator. Some people become savants after a blow to the head or an epileptic fit – but don't bash yourself on the head in the hope of becoming a savant! Other savants are born with this ability. Their special skills, often in mathematics or music, baffle scientists and challenge our ideas about intelligence.

SPOTTING PATTERNS

Some people have an amazing ability to know the solutions to difficult sums very quickly. A few of these people are 'savants' (see box above), but others just spot patterns and use shortcuts to find the answers.

As a young boy, the German mathematician Carl Friedrich Gauss annoyed his mathematics teacher by being able to give the answer in seconds when set the task of adding up the numbers 1 to 100. The teacher had hoped to have a rest while the children worked it out, but Gauss saw immediately that the answer is:

$$50 \times (100 + 1) = 5050$$

How does it work? Think of the numbers 1 to 100 written in a long line and then fold the line in half so that 1 is above 100. If you add up each of these pairs you get 101 every time (see below). There are 50 pairs, so the answer is 101 x 50 = 5050. There will always be half as many sums as the number you are adding up to, as you have folded the line in half.

3 22 21 20 19 18 17 16 15 14 13 (12) 11 10 9 8 (7) 6 5 4 3 2 (1)

79 80 81 82 83 84 85 86 87 88 (89) 90 91 92 93 (94) 95 96 97 98 99 (100)

To find the sum of the numbers 1–100, imagine that they're on a long piece of paper.

Look at the pattern of number 5s on the far left. Someone with synesthesia who sees numbers as colours would see it very differently. He or she might immediately spot the six number 2s forming a triangle inside the pattern.

People with synesthesia have different senses from everyone else. They may see numbers and words as colours or shapes, or hear them as sounds, and may experience sounds as colours. The synesthetic savant, Daniel Tammet can carry out complicated calculations in an instant and recall the first 20,000 digits of pi (3.141...) – see page 104. When he has a sum to work out, he sees the shapes and colours that represent the numbers, watches them rearrange themselves and then knows the answer to the question.

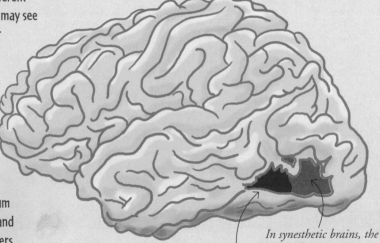

This is the region of the brain used to recognize words and numbers

In synesthetic brains, the region for recognizing colour might be triggered at the same time

GENIUS!

Looking at Gauss's sum again, you can call the number you're adding up to n, we can use a special way of writing down the calculation. Instead of writing 50 x (100 + 1), if we use n in place of 100 we can write ½n x (n + 1). This is a formula. It is true for all numbers – just put the number you want in place of 'n' and you solve it.

11-TIMES TRICK

There are a few other patterns that can help you do really quick calculations and look very smart!

Take a look at these patterns in the 11-times table. Do you notice anything special in the numbers?

$$11 \times 11 = 121$$
$$11 \times 12 = 132$$
$$11 \times 13 = 143$$
$$...$$
$$11 \times 71 = 781$$

The number you're multiplying by, makes up the outside digits of your solution :

$$11 \times 71 = 7...1$$

The digit in the middle of your solution is the sum of the two digits in the second number:

$$7 + 1 = 8, \text{ so } 11 \times 71 = 781$$

You can write this as a formula as well:

$$11 \times ab = a[a + b]b$$

EVEN SMARTER

If the numbers added together (a plus b) come to more than 10, add 1 to the first digit in the answer. Just like this:

$$11 \times 79 = 7...9,$$

with 7 + 9 = 16 to go in the middle, so it's

$$(7 + 1)69, \text{ or } 869$$

MORE TRICKS

To work out any number times 10, you just need to add a zero to the end of the number:

$$75 \times 10 = 750$$

To multiply by 5, add a zero and then halve the number – so you're multiplying by 10 first and then dividing by 2:

$$75 \times 5 = 750 \div 2 = 375$$

To multiply by 9, multiply by 10 and then subtract the number once:

$$9 \times 78 = (10 \times 78) - 78 = 780 - 78 = 702$$

see for yourself

See how quickly you can work out the sum of the numbers 1 to 700.

Answer:
½ x 700 x (700 + 1) = 350 x 701 = 245,350

31

8 HOW TO PREDICT A COMET

Comets puzzled and frightened people for thousands of years because they appeared in the sky for a while and then disappeared. They were thought to be warnings of terrible events about to happen. It turned out that some comets are regular visitors and we can work out when they will visit again – and they don't bring terrible events.

MOVING STARS

If you watch the stars at night, you will see that they seem to move around slowly. Some of the bright, shiny things that look like stars are actually planets, which all move in their own paths, or orbits, around the Sun. The rest of the stars seem to move together, but in fact it is Earth going round that creates this effect, so we are moving relative to them. Early astronomers struggled with this idea, largely because they thought Earth was at the centre of the Universe.

Even when astronomers came up with a model of the Universe to make their theory work, comets came along and messed it all up. The first mention of a comet dates from 4,300 years ago in China.

A comet appears in the sky, moves slowly across it, and disappears again. So how can we know when it will come back, so that we can prepare for it?

Knowing when comets are due to return can warn of a collision with Earth.

FREQUENT AND INFREQUENT VISITORS

Some comets 'live' quite nearby. They stay fairly close to the Sun, so they come back quite frequently. Others live a very long way away and so are rarely seen. Astronomers divide comets into short-period comets and non-periodic comets. Short-period comets visit at least once every 200 years and have predictable orbits. Other comets return less frequently, or perhaps not at all, and are much harder to predict.

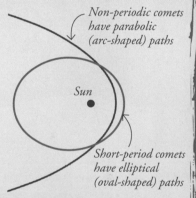

Non-periodic comets have parabolic (arc-shaped) paths

Sun

Short-period comets have elliptical (oval-shaped) paths

Encke's Comet returns more often than any other; it has an orbit of 3.3 years, so it is visible every 40 months. We do not know which comet has the longest orbit as it's impossible to tell with some. Maybe they are dragged in towards the Sun just once on their way to somewhere else – or maybe they have an oval orbit that takes thousands of years to complete.

ROUND AND ROUND

Comets that have a short return period orbit the Sun in an ellipse (oval). They come back regularly, so they are easy to predict. Edmond Halley first predicted a comet's return. He worked on one of the most famous comets, now called Halley's Comet. He noticed that its path across the sky in 1682 was like that of a comet seen in 1607 – and that the 1607 comet was like one in 1531. He decided it was the same comet coming back at fairly regular intervals:

1682 – 1607 = 75 years
1607 – 1531 = 76 years

He predicted that the comet would return in 1759, and it did – but Halley had died 16 years earlier.

When you know the comet's return period, it is easy to spot it reappearing through history. Halley's comet was present at the Battle of Hastings in 1066 and was last seen in 1986. It is due again in 2061.

This is a drawing of Halley's Comet as it is shown in the Bayeaux Tapestry, which tells the story of the Battle of Hastings in 1066.

The best wine

Wine that was produced in years when a 'great comet' appeared is said to be of exceptional quality. Winemakers say that unexplained effects of the comet on the weather and the atmosphere are responsible. Wine from the years 1811, 1826, 1839, 1845, 1852, 1858, 1861, 1985 and 1989 are some of the best of the last 200 years and all coincide with a significant comet. Whether or not there is really a relationship between comets and wines is a question about correlations (see pages 160–161).

SLING-SHOT COMETS

The great mathematician Sir Isaac Newton thought all comets came from outside the Solar System. He thought they were attracted to the Sun by gravity, whizzed around it, and shot off back into space never to return, or to return only after a very long time. Newton explained how to work out the path of such a comet from its position in the sky, recorded on three occasions over two months. He plotted the path of the 1680 Great Comet, which won't be back until 11037.

Comets that 'live' a long way away have odd orbits because planets' gravity affects their paths. Comet Hyakutake has increased its return time from 17,000 years to 70,000 years. It last visited in 1996. Comet Kohoutek appeared in 1973 on its first visit in 150,000 years, and will come back in 75,000 years… so don't wait up!

Comet Hale-Bopp was visible to the naked eye for a record 18 months (1996–1997), twice as long as the previous record holder, the Great Comet of 1811.

see for yourself

The comet Faye was last brightest in October 2006, and before that it was last brightest in January 1999. When will it next appear?

Answer:
It has a return period of nearly eight years, so it will be visible in July 2014.

35

HOW TO FOOL YOUR FRIENDS

Lots of people are not very good at mathematics – or at least they think they aren't. This gives you the chance to astound them with some really impressive number tricks.

THINK OF A NUMBER

Try this trick on a friend – you can pretend that you are a mind reader. Ask your friend to think of a three-digit number with all three digits the same, such as 333 or 777. Add up the digits and divide the number you first thought of by this amount – so 333 divided by 9, for instance. The answer is always 37. How does it work? Let's use n to stand for the digit that is tripled, so the number would be written nnn. This number is really $100n + 10n + n$, which is $111n$. (Think about it: $333 = 300 + 30 + 3$.) When you add up the digits, the sum is $3n$. When you divide $111n$ by $3n$, the answer is 37, because $37 \times 3 = 111$.

see for yourself

Can you work out this one?

Add another five lines to make nine.

Answer:
Use the extra lines to change the lines into letters: NINE.

MAKE UP YOUR OWN NUMBER TRICKS

Simple number tricks often work by writing the chosen number out of the question. Here's an example.

Choose a number from 1 to 10	4
Double the number	8
Add 10 to the answer	18
Divide the answer by 2	9
Subtract the number you started with	5
The answer is always 5	

To see how this works, let's swap the chosen number for the letter n and write it out as sums:

Choose a number from 1 to 10	n
Double the number	$2n$
Add 10 to the answer	$2n + 10$
Divide the answer by 2	$n + 5$
Subtract the number you started with	5
The answer is always 5	

There have to be enough steps in the trick for the person you are playing it on not to notice that they've abandoned their original number.

37

HAPPY BIRTHDAY

This is an interesting trick to try out on your friends as it's quite hard to see how it works. You will probably need a pen and paper to work this out as there are quite a few steps.

Tell your friend to take the month of their birthday and multiply the number by five – so if they were born in February, for example, they would multiply 5 x 2.

Then add 7 and multiply by 4.

Then add 13 and multiply by 5.

Now tell your friend to add the date of the day they were born.

Finally, subtract the magic number 205. The number that is left should be the month of their birthday followed by the day. Here is an example, using a birthday of March 6.

Next to it are formulas to show you how each step can work for any birthday, with *d* representing the day and *m* the month.

$5 \times 3 = 15$	$5 \times m = 5m$
$15 + 7 = 22$	$5m + 7$
$22 \times 4 = 88$	$(5m + 7) \times 4 = 20m + 28$
$88 + 13 = 101$	$20m + 28 + 13 = 20m + 41$
$101 \times 5 = 505$	$(20m + 41) \times 5 = 100m + 205$
$505 + 6 = 511$	$100m + d + 205$
$511 - 205 = 306$	$100m + d$
306 is 3 (March) and 06 (the date)	

You can test different birthdays with the formula $100m + d$ to see how this will work.

If you were born on November 28, the final solution would be: $1,100 + 28 = 1,128$.
If you were born on January 2, it would be: $100 + 2 = 102$.

DIGIT SWITCH

Here's another number trick to wow your friends. Write down a two-digit number that has two different digits (so not 44 or 77, for instance). Reverse the digits. Subtract the smaller number from the bigger number. Swap the digits around again. Add the last two numbers together. The answer is always 99.

Make your audience work!

Some number games trick the audience into using numbers you choose. Try this one. Take the current year – such as 2014 – and double it (4028). Write this down, and put it in an envelope.

Now ask a friend to think of their age, and the date of any memorable historical event, then add these two numbers together. (For example: 12 + 1914 = 1926.) Next they have to add the year they were born to the number of years that have passed since the event they thought of. (So 2002 + 100 = 2102). Now they have to add both results together – and then you open the envelope to reveal the answer!

This will always work as the audience has to work with two sums that both add up to the current year: their date of birth and age, and the date of an event and the years that have passed since.

HOW TO DO SUPER-FAST SUMS

It's impressive when people can come up with a rough answer to a hard mathematics question really quickly – but this is a trick you can learn easily. It's all about rounding.

'IT'S ABOUT...'

A teacher asks you to carry a bag of 413 balls that each weighs 40 g. Will you be able to pick it up? The quickest way to get some idea is to round the number of balls down to 400: 400 x 40 g = 16,000 g = 16 kg. It's about half of an average child's weight – so you'll have to get help!

How close is your estimated figure? Now work out the true weight of the balls: 413 x 40 g = 16,520 g. So you were quite close. The trick is in rounding the numbers well enough to start with. If you had rounded up to 500 balls you would be a long way out: 500 x 40 g = 20,000 g = 20 kg.

Do you count all of the balls individually or take a best guess and round the number up or down?

MAKE IT WORK FOR YOU!

If you're doing a rough calculation, make sure you don't cheat yourself! Generally, if there are two figures, round one up and one down. But if it's going to make a difference to you if the figure is too high (or too low), round in your favour. Suppose your father asks you to help him do some gardening and says he'll give you 33 jelly beans an hour, but he will pay you only in whole packets of ten jelly beans. You work 3 hours and 20 minutes. Are you going to round that down to 30 jelly beans an hour for 3 hours and accept just 90? You could round it down to 30 an hour and up to 4 hours (120) or up to 40 an hour and down to 3 hours (also 120). You should be getting nearly 110 for 3 hours 20 minutes at 33 an hour, so you can get an extra ten if you get the rounding right!

YOU USE ROUNDING ALL THE TIME!

Rounding isn't cheating - you do it all the time. If someone asks how old you are, you say '11' or '10' - you don't say '10 years and 5 months and 13 days'. Often, an approximate answer is good enough. It's all to do with knowing how accurate you need to be. You wouldn't measure your weight to the last milligram, or your height to a millimetre. Rounding is just being relaxed about numbers.

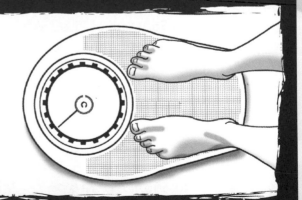

Do you want to own a private yacht and a swimming pool the size of a lake? Mathematics can help you – successful businesses are built on a solid foundation of number-crunching.

MAKING A PROFIT

You've probably noticed that you can buy similar items for very different prices. Are shoes that cost £500 really a hundred times better than those that cost £5? No, they are a bit better, but not a hundred times better! A shop fixes its prices using mathematics and psychology – knowledge about the way people think. If you buy shoes for £5, you're pleased with the bargain. And buying shoes for £500 is all about the label and the image. Everyone's happy – especially the shops.

A business makes a profit by selling things for more than it costs to make or buy them. If a pair of shoes costs a shop £8 and it sells them for £15, the profit is:

$$£15 - £8 = £7$$

A shop can sell more items at a low price, but it makes less profit on each one. At a high price, it makes more on each sale but doesn't sell as many. Setting the right price to make the most money takes skill – and mathematics.

SELLING OUT

Some businesses sell special versions of things that cost a lot more than a normal version. These often sell out quickly. There's always a waiting list for really expensive sports cars, for instance. By setting a high price, the manufacturer makes the car more desirable.

FIND YOUR LEVEL

Suppose one shop sells those £8 shoes for £10, making a profit of £2. It sells 400 pairs, so the profit is 400 x £2 = £800. Another shop sells the same shoes for £20 a pair, making £12 profit. It sells only 100 pairs, but the total profit is £1,200. This second shop has made more money by selling fewer pairs.

DON'T GO TOO LOW!

Imagine a supermarket that buys beans for 30p a tin. When the beans are priced at 35p a tin, they sell 1,000 tins a week, making a profit of £50. When they price them at 31p a tin, they sell 7,000 tins a week, making £70 profit. At 28p a tin, they sell 10,000 tins a week, but they lose 2p on each tin, making a loss of £200. So that really doesn't sound like a good idea!

12 HOW TO CONTACT AN ALIEN

There might be as many as three septillion stars in the Universe – that's three followed by 24 zeroes. What are the chances that Earth is the only planet with intelligent life? Pretty small, according to some scientists. With the help of mathematics, we might eventually be able to talk to intelligent beings on other planets.

OVER AND OUT

Radio waves travel at the speed of light, so at the moment they are the fastest way we have of sending a message, and our best way of signalling to other worlds. But the Universe is full of natural radio waves produced by stars and left over from the Big Bang that created the Universe. To use radio waves to contact any aliens we will have to make sure our messages don't look like background noise.

Mathematics is the same all over the Universe, so it might just be the ideal means of communication!

DO YOU SPEAK SUMS?

If an alien civilization has developed to the point where it is looking at radio waves, its citizens will have the same ideas about what is a pattern and what is random as we do. They will be able to work out that the messages we send are not just the mumbling of a pulsar or the shout of a supernova.

ANSWERING BACK

Distances in space are so huge that even radio waves take a long time to get anywhere useful. They take 8.5 minutes just to get to the Sun, and 4.2 years to

HOW RADIO WORKS

Radio waves are a type of energy that can be beamed through space. Like all waves of energy, the radio waves have a wavelength and a frequency. When a radio tunes into one station, its receiver is just picking up an input of one wavelength-frequency pair. The amplitude of the wave varies. These changes in the amplitude carry the information that the radio turns into a signal, which tells its speakers what to to play.

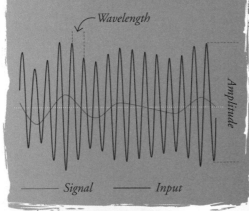

Wavelength

Amplitude

——— Signal   ——— Input

get to the next nearest star. If the closest intelligent aliens are 40 light years away, it will take 40 years for our radio messages to get to them. If an alien 40 light years away picks up our signal, and sends a reply immediately, it will take another 40 years for the answer to get back to us.

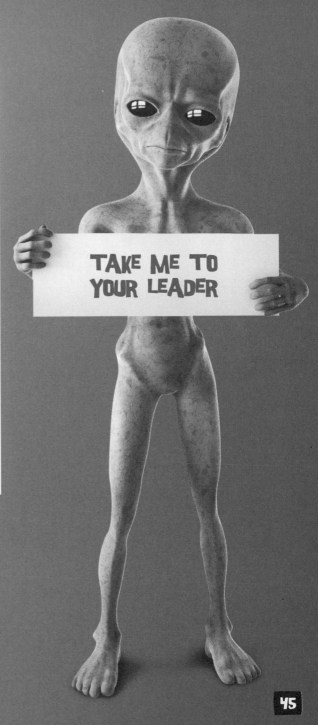

TAKE ME TO YOUR LEADER

As well as the messages we send into space deliberately, radio waves we produce as TV and radio broadcasts and mobile phone signals all leak out into space to some extent. Aliens won't be listening to the latest news as it won't have got far enough yet – but the first radio news show was broadcast in 1920, so some stories might have got far enough to have been noticed. An alien 70 light years away might just be catching up with the Second World War.

The world's first regular television broadcasts didn't begin until 1929. Who knows what any aliens will make of today's TV programmes by the time they get all the way to them?

What are the chances?

Astronomer Frank Drake wrote a formula, or equation, to work out the number of findable alien civilizations in our galaxy, the Milky Way. Unfortunately, we don't yet know any of the numbers to fill in to get an answer, but the mathematics is ready for when we do. The equation looks like this:

Number of civilizations in the Milky Way we could communicate with

The average number of stars formed per year

The number of civilizations that develop a technology that releases signs of their existence into space

$$N = R^* \times f_p \times n_e \times f_\ell \times f_i \times f_c \times L$$

The number of those stars with planets

The average number of planets that could support life that those stars have

The number of those planets that develop life

The number of those that develop intelligent life

The length of time for which they release those signs

MESSAGE IN A BOTTLE

Radio waves are not our only hope of contacting aliens. Two Pioneer spacecraft launched in 1972 and 1973 have metal plaques showing humans, our position in the Solar System and the Milky Way, and the structure of the hydrogen atom. Two Voyager spacecraft launched in 1977 carry gold discs with recordings of sounds from Earth, including language and animal noises, photographs and scientific and mathematical information. Any alien who found these would know that they were made by intelligent beings.

The spacecraft Voyager 1 is 17 billion km (10.6 billion miles) from the Sun, heading into deep space. Maybe it will be seen by an alien spacecraft, also out looking for other life in the Universe.

The Milky Way is 100,000 light years in diameter, so aliens on one side would have to wait a very long time for news from the other side!

see for yourself

At the same time as sending out radio signals, we are scanning the skies for radio evidence of aliens. If you would like to help look for possible aliens by finding patterns in radio data collected from space, go to http://setiathome.ssl.berkeley.edu.

13 HOW TO CRACK A CODE

For as long as there have been people writing secret messages, there have been others trying to crack the codes! Mathematicians have very logical brains, and they are often employed as code-crackers during a war.

SIMPLE CODES

Substitution codes (where one letter or symbol is swapped for another) are the easiest to crack, especially those that just go backwards or forwards in the alphabet by a few letters. Even if a substitution code uses random letters or symbols, you can unravel it. Look at the message shown across the bottom of these pages.

What you know about the English language will help you to crack the code. There are two one-letter words, Z and V. In English, there are only two one-letter

words, 'a' and 'I'. So you know that Z must be either A or I, and V must be the other. Now to the two- and three-letter words. The most common three-letter words in English are 'the' and 'and'. The word 'BOM' appears twice in this message. It cannot be 'and' because we know A is either Z or V, so let us guess that it's 'the'. That gives us three more letters: B = T, O = H and M = E. Putting these letters in the message gives:

I JAt the leP Yet Oellase i* a N9ttSe i* a Na$
or
A JAt the leP Yet Oelli$e a* I N9ttSe a*i NiS

Z JAB BOM IMPYMB OMI IVSM

'A* I' could be 'as I' but there are more possibilities for 'I* A'. A two-letter word starting with I can only be 'is', 'it', 'if' or 'in'. 'It a' doesn't make sense and 'is a' and 'if a' would probably not occur again two words later, so you could try * = N:

I JAt the IePYet Oella$e in a N9ttSe in a Na$

A word can't have four vowels in a row (Oella$e) so 'I' must be a consonant.

HOW OFTEN?

In any language, some letters are used more than others. Looking at how often a letter crops up is called frequency analysis. In English, 'E' is used most. Of the consonants, 'S' is used a great deal, as is 'T'. So, I could be S. That would give us:

I JAt the sePYet Oessa$e in a N9ttSe in a Na$

Now you have got enough to start making guesses and trying letters out. The longer the message, the easier it is to crack as you have more patterns to look at. The answer is on page 51.

The answer is on page 51.

RECRUITING CODE-BREAKERS

During wars, governments and armies try to persuade people who might be good at cracking codes to work for them. In the Second World War, the British government recruited mathematicians and people who did crosswords in the newspaper. People like this are good at seeing patterns in strings of letters and numbers.

Z   V N9BBSM Z   V NV$

MACHINE CODES

During the Second World War, the German armed forces used machines to code messages. The Enigma machine looked a bit like a typewriter. It had lots of different settings that were changed each day, and these controlled which letters came out when a coder typed in a message. The code was difficult to crack without knowing the settings because there were about 15,000,000,000,000,000,000 (15 billion billion) possible settings for even the simplest Enigma machine.

The first programmable computer was developed at Bletchley Park, England. It was designed to crack the Enigma codes used by the German forces during the Second World War. Even a modern computer would take months to crack an Enigma code if it worked by just trying out one combination of letters after another. Instead, the Bletchley computer looked for patterns that could lead it to pairs or groups of letters that turn up often in words (German words, of course!).

CRACKING ANCIENT LANGUAGES

It's not just secret messages that can be understood using code-breaking techniques – we can also learn to read languages that nobody knows anymore. Ancient languages are some of the hardest codes to crack. Without a copy of a text in a second language, there are no clues. Some of the most talented code-crackers have worked on cracking ancient writing systems.

The ancient Egyptians wrote using a system of pictures called hieroglyphs. Nobody knew what these hieroglyphs

An Enigma machine was used like a typewriter, but created a coded message.

meant until the discovery of the Rosetta Stone in 1799. This engraved stone had the same message in three languages, including hieroglyphs and ancient Greek, which people could read. They were able to use the Greek to translate the hieroglyphs and crack the ancient code.

Uncrackable computer codes

Modern computers encrypt secret data, such as banking details, converting it into a code. The method of coding uses very large prime numbers – numbers that cannot be divided by any numbers except themselves and 1. Examples of small prime numbers are 7, 11 and 13.

Two large prime numbers are multiplied together and the answer is used as the basis of the code. The same primes are needed to decode the message. If the prime numbers have five digits, then there are about 1.1 trillion possible results to the encryption. If the prime has 16 digits, it would take a modern super-computer 11,000 quadrillion years to crack the code by trying out possibilities. That is longer than most people are prepared to wait.

The secret message reads:
I put the secret message in a bottle in a bag.

14 HOW TO WRITE A SECRET MESSAGE

People have always kept secrets and they have written in secret codes for thousands of years. You don't have to be a spy to use a code to send messages or write a secret diary that only you can read. Just remember how your code works – you don't want to have to try to crack your own code because you have forgotten how to decode it.

CAESAR'S WAY

Even Romans sent secret messages. Julius Caesar invented a code called the Caesar cipher 2,000 years ago. It swapped one letter for another – a type of code called a substitution code (see page 48). Swap each letter for the one that comes three after it in the alphabet.

So: **I lost the secret map**
becomes
L orvw wkh vhfuhw pds

You can shift the code by any number of letters, backwards or forwards. There are only 25 possible swaps using shifts because there are 26 letters (and the sequence in which A = A is not very secret!). For a code that is harder to crack, you could pick random letters for each letter of the alphabet. There are 26 x 25 x 24 x… x 2 x 1 possible sequences. This very big number is called 'factorial 26' and is written !26.

NOT JUST LETTERS

In the 16th century, Mary Queen of Scots was plotting to overthrow Queen Elizabeth I. She wrote her plans in a code where each letter was represented by a different symbol. Another substitution code is Braille – a system of raised dots used in books for blind people. It uses a pattern of six dots that can be present (raised) or absent. As there are six dots and two possible states, there are 2 x 2 x 2 x 2 x 2 x 2 = 64 possible letters (we multiply by 2 for each dot).

GIVE THEM SOME STICK

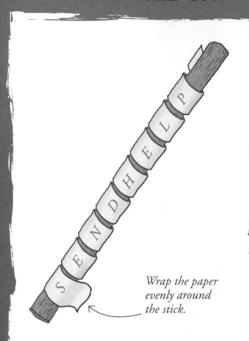

Wrap the paper evenly around the stick.

A very old way of sending a secret message uses a long strip of paper and a stick. Wrap the paper around the stick, then write your message along the stick, putting one letter on the paper for each turn. Unwrap the paper and fill in the gaps with random letters. To make it harder for anyone else to crack your message, vary the spacing of the letters so that the interval between the 'real' letters is irregular. To read your message, a person has to wrap it around a stick that's the same size so that the letters line up again.

SECRET SQUARES

Substitution codes are easy to crack, but there is a better way to keep your secrets safe. You will need a grid of 26 x 26 squares with the letters A–Z written along the top row and down the first column.

The rest of the rows should then include the other letters of the alphabet, as shown in the grid below.

Agree a code phrase with your friend. Let's use the phrase 'shark attack'.

Code phrase letter

Message letter you want to encode

	a	b	c	d	e	f	g	h	i	j	k	l	m	n	o	p	q	r	s	t	u	v	w	x	y	z
a	b	c	d	e	f	g	h	i	j	k	l	m	n	o	p	q	r	s	t	u	v	w	x	y	z	a
b	c	d	e	f	g	h	i	j	k	l	m	n	o	p	q	r	s	t	u	v	w	x	y	z	a	b
c	d	e	f	g	h	i	j	k	l	m	n	o	p	q	r	s	t	u	v	w	x	y	z	a	b	c
d	e	f	g	h	i	j	k	l	m	n	o	p	q	r	s	t	u	v	w	x	y	z	a	b	c	d
e	f	g	h	i	j	k	l	m	n	o	p	q	r	s	t	u	v	w	x	y	z	a	b	c	d	e
f	g	h	i	j	k	l	m	n	o	p	q	r	s	t	u	v	w	x	y	z	a	b	c	d	e	f
g	h	i	j	k	l	m	n	o	p	q	r	s	t	u	v	w	x	y	z	a	b	c	d	e	f	g
h	i	j	k	l	m	n	o	p	q	r	s	t	u	v	w	x	y	z	a	b	c	d	e	f	g	h
i	j	k	l	m	n	o	p	q	r	s	t	u	v	w	x	y	z	a	b	c	d	e	f	g	h	i
j	k	l	m	n	o	p	q	r	s	t	u	v	w	x	y	z	a	b	c	d	e	f	g	h	i	j
k	l	m	n	o	p	q	r	s	t	u	v	w	x	y	z	a	b	c	d	e	f	g	h	i	j	k
l	m	n	o	p	q	r	s	t	u	v	w	x	y	z	a	b	c	d	e	f	g	h	i	j	k	l
m	n	o	p	q	r	s	t	u	v	w	x	y	z	a	b	c	d	e	f	g	h	i	j	k	l	m
n	o	p	q	r	s	t	u	v	w	x	y	z	a	b	c	d	e	f	g	h	i	j	k	l	m	n
o	p	q	r	s	t	u	v	w	x	y	z	a	b	c	d	e	f	g	h	i	j	k	l	m	n	o
p	q	r	s	t	u	v	w	x	y	z	a	b	c	d	e	f	g	h	i	j	k	l	m	n	o	p
q	r	s	t	u	v	w	x	y	z	a	b	c	d	e	f	g	h	i	j	k	l	m	n	o	p	q
r	s	t	u	v	w	x	y	z	a	b	c	d	e	f	g	h	i	j	k	l	m	n	o	p	q	r
s	t	u	v	w	x	y	z	a	b	c	d	e	f	g	h	i	j	k	l	m	n	o	p	q	r	s
t	u	v	w	x	y	z	a	b	c	d	e	f	g	h	i	j	k	l	m	n	o	p	q	r	s	t
u	v	w	x	y	z	a	b	c	d	e	f	g	h	i	j	k	l	m	n	o	p	q	r	s	t	u
v	w	x	y	z	a	b	c	d	e	f	g	h	i	j	k	l	m	n	o	p	q	r	s	t	u	v
w	x	y	z	a	b	c	d	e	f	g	h	i	j	k	l	m	n	o	p	q	r	s	t	u	v	w
x	y	z	a	b	c	d	e	f	g	h	i	j	k	l	m	n	o	p	q	r	s	t	u	v	w	x
y	z	a	b	c	d	e	f	g	h	i	j	k	l	m	n	o	p	q	r	s	t	u	v	w	x	y
z	a	b	c	d	e	f	g	h	i	j	k	l	m	n	o	p	q	r	s	t	u	v	w	x	y	z

S H A R	K A	T T A	C K S H	A R	K A T	T A C K S H
come	to	the	park	at	two	oclock
U V M V	O O	M A E	R K J R	A K	O W H	K C N Y U R

Write out the message you want to encode and then write the code phrase above it so that the letters line up. Repeat the code phrase as necessary.

Look up each letter pair in the alphabet square. For the first letter in this message, you would look down the S column until you come to the C row and read off the letter in the square. (Column S and row C give the same letter as column C and row S.) To decode the message, your friend needs to write the key phrase above it and look up the letters again.

This code is hard to break because each time you use a letter in your message, it comes out as a different letter in code.

☞ To translate the coded message (in red), your friend needs to write out the code phrase ('shark attack') above it and draw the same letter grid. He or she starts with the S column and reads down until he or she comes to the U. At the U, your friend reads across to the first column to see which letter U stands for – in this case C.

Leonardo's mirror

Leonardo da Vinci was an Italian artist and scientist who lived in the 16th century. He painted the famous *Mona Lisa* and designed ingenious machines – including a helicopter and a submarine. He wrote all his notebooks in code, but not a very difficult code to crack. He wrote in mirror writing, which means he wrote from right to left, writing each word and letter backwards, which looked like this:

If we wrote the first sentence of this box in mirror writing, it would look like this:

Leonardo da Vinci was an Italian artist and scientist who lived in the 16th century.

see for yourself

Invent a code of your own using a pattern of dots, squares, or lines, like Braille. How many possible letters could you make?

15 HOW TO WIN A RACE

If you run really fast, you can win a race – or so you would think. But in mathematics this can be tricky to explain and is called a paradox.

ACHILLES AND THE TORTOISE

The Greek mathematician Zeno lived about 2,500 years ago. He used this story to explain a paradox – a situation that seems to go against common sense or our experience of the world. A tortoise challenged the god Achilles to a race. Achilles could run very quickly, so he laughed. The tortoise claimed that as long as Achilles gave him a head start – 10 m (33 ft) would be enough – the tortoise could win, and he could prove by logic that he would win.

Zeno describes another paradox, which he claims proves that movement does not exist. But we know things DO move.

In Zeno's arrow paradox it says that if he shoots an arrow, we can say exactly where the arrow is at a time we call 'now'. So at any moment the arrow is still and is neither moving to where it is, nor to where it is not.

Time is made up of an infinite sequence of instants, or 'nows', in which the position of the arrow is fixed.

So how can the arrow ever go anywhere? Mathematicians believe that the answer has to be that the arrow somehow moves between the 'nows'.

Achilles asked him for proof. The tortoise explained that while Achilles was covering the first 10 m (33 ft), he would be moving ahead, perhaps gaining another metre. It would not take Achilles long to cover that extra metre, but even as he did so, the tortoise would move further on. And while Achilles covered the next little bit to catch up with him, the tortoise would have moved another, even shorter distance. There would never be a point at which Achilles could overtake the tortoise, because as soon as he caught up with the tortoise's position, the tortoise would be a little further ahead. So how could Achilles ever catch up with the tortoise?

IN A MOMENT OF TIME

Zeno's paradox treats both distance and time as though they can be divided into ever smaller parts. So the only way of answering the question of how Achilles beat the tortoise is to say that both distance and time cannot, in fact, be divided into ever smaller portions. There has to be a smallest distance and a smallest instant of time. In this tiny moment of time, Achilles can move further than the tortoise. Scale this up, and it means that Achilles is allowed to run faster than the tortoise and that he will win the race.

16 HOW TO SWAT A FLY

The way we draw graphs today developed from a mathematician lying in bed and being annoyed by a fly. So we could say that a simple fly, dead for 300 years, led to a revolution in mathematics.

LAZY MATHEMATICIAN MEETS ANNOYING FLY

The French thinker René Descartes liked to do most of his work while lying in his bed. Luckily his work involved thinking about problems in science, mathematics and philosophy rather than building bridges!

One day, Descartes was lying in his bed watching a fly buzz around the room, when he realized that he could say exactly where the fly was at any point. He could pinpoint the fly's position by giving its distance in three directions from a corner of the room, either at the floor or ceiling. The idea of giving three distances to define a point developed into the system of using coordinates in geometry. These are called Cartesian coordinates, after René Descartes.

If coordinate geometry was useful just for saying where a fly was, it would not be very famous. Luckily, it can be used for lots of things, from solving equations to discovering trends in data and drawing shapes. We can define a shape by giving the coordinates of its points and then joining them with lines. For anything but the simplest shape, this is much easier than giving the length of each line and the size of each angle. We can solve problems by drawing graphs from data or equations, and discover patterns in numbers that might look like just a random jumble when written down.

ONE FLY, ONE WALL

The simplest way of watching the fly is to see it against a single wall. Its position can be specified by saying how far up from the floor it is and how far across from the corner. This is shown in a graph, like the one on the right, with two axes, labelled x (going along the floor) and y (going up the wall).

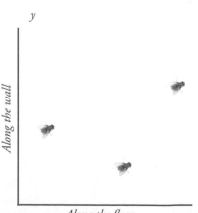

y

Along the wall

Along the floor

x

ADDING NEGATIVE NUMBERS

What if the fly went downstairs? It would be below the floor, so we'd have to add negative numbers to the graph to show this. And if it went outside, or into another room, it could go further to the left than the wall. Again, we can add a negative scale so that it can go past the zero point of the corner of the room.

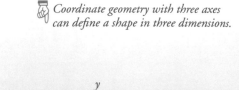

Coordinate geometry with three axes can define a shape in three dimensions.

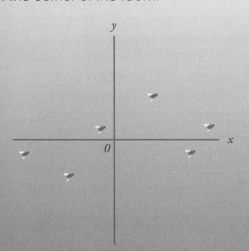

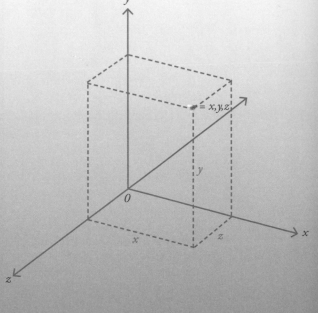

3D SPACE

As long as the fly walks across the surface of the wall, two axes are enough to give its exact position and it becomes easy to swat. The trouble with flies, though, is that they move around. Using just the x- and y-axes we cannot tell how far away from the wall the fly is. For that, we need an axis that comes out of the page towards us (positive) and goes into the paper away from us (negative). This is equivalent to how far into the room – or outside the window – the fly has gone.

Now we can say where exactly in space the fly is by giving three numbers. The corner of the room from where Descartes measured his fly's position, is called the 'origin' in the coordinate system. At this point, the fly's coordinates are (0,0,0).

The problem is that flies are most annoying when they are buzzing around. You can use 3D coordinate geometry to say exactly where the fly is at any one moment, but to track its path as it buzzes around the room, you would need to plot it in these three dimensions and time. We cannot do this by drawing the path on paper as we can with three dimensions, but it is still a useful thing to do (and not just for working out where a fly is). Lots of things have to be traced or planned through time as well as space, from the path of a spacecraft to a firework display or animated characters in a film.

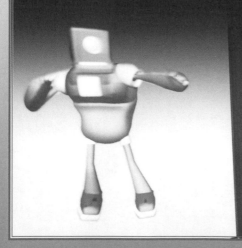

Sensors pick up the model's movement and project it as 3D animation.

If the fly moves to the right, up or out towards us, its coordinates on the x-, y- or z-axis are positive. If it moves to the left, down or back away from us, its coordinates are negative.

So, using these three coordinates, you can say exactly where the fly is and with a good shot, you can swat it.

17 HOW TO PAINT A MASTERPIECE

There's more to painting a great picture than you might expect. It's best if you have a bit of artistic talent – but talent alone is not enough. Mathematics has helped artists for thousands of years.

THE GOLDEN RATIO

Remember Fibonacci and his rabbits (see page 22)? Dividing one Fibonacci number by the next one gives a result of about 0.618. This amazing number crops up throughout nature and 1:0.618 is called the 'golden ratio'. A ratio is the relationship between two numbers. A ratio of 2:1 means the first number is twice as big as the other.

HOW TO DRAW A GOLDEN RECTANGLE

A golden rectangle has sides in the proportion 1: 0.618, so if one side was 1 m (39 in), the other would be 61.8 cm (24 in). You can draw a golden rectangle very easily. Start by drawing a square. Now draw a line from halfway along the bottom of the square to one of the top corners. Use this to set a pair of compasses to form half the width, or radius, of a circle. Now draw through the two corners of the square (1). Extend the bottom side of the square until it meets the edge of the circle. That gives you the long side of the rectangle. Now you can draw in the other sides (2).

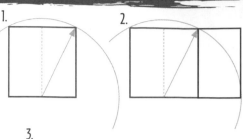

1.
2.

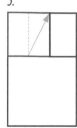

3.

If you now draw a square beneath the rectangle's longer side, you will get a new golden rectangle (3).

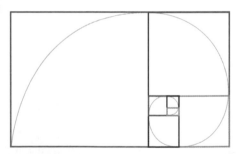

Using this method, you can draw many more larger and larger golden rectangles. If you then draw a spiral through the corners of the golden rectangles, it produces exactly the same spiral that you can see in sunflower heads, pineapples and pine cones.

☞ *Why is the* Mona Lisa *still so popular? Maybe because her face fits perfectly into a golden rectangle!*

WHAT A MONA!

The proportions of the golden ratio seem to appeal to our sense of balance: rectangles and spirals based on it appear in art and architecture from all places and times. The face of Leonardo da Vinci's *Mona Lisa* fits into a golden rectangle, for example.

Great artists don't just position their subjects right in the centre of a picture. The best paintings often have the subject slightly off to the side, or up or down a bit. Artists and photographers often use the 'rule of thirds' to help work out their composition. If the most interesting part of a picture is in the middle, your eye is drawn straight to that and nothing else. But if the main subject is offset by a third in any direction, the picture is more interesting and you look around it properly.

PUTTING THINGS IN PERSPECTIVE

Very old paintings don't look like real life. In the real world, things that are close to us look bigger than things that are farther away. This is called perspective. Before the 15th century, pictures often showed people and objects as bigger or smaller depending on how important they were. Of course, what we see isn't always what's actually 'true' – the parallel lines that are the sides of a road seem to meet in the distance, and a person seems to get smaller as he or she walks away. Paintings that look realistic copy these effects, but they have to get the 'wrongness' just right to look convincing.

Paintings that use perspective use one, two or more vanishing points. These are the points at which perspective lines meet in the picture. Vanishing points copy the way we see the world. If you look at railway tracks going off into the distance, the tracks seem to come to a point on the horizon. That is the vanishing point.

ODD NUMBERS

Great artists know that a picture works best if it shows odd numbers of items, as it's harder for the eye and mind to fit odd numbers of items into neat groups. Instead, we spend longer looking at a picture with three, five or seven objects.

IT TAKES ALL SORTS

Varying the sizes and shapes of objects in a picture also holds our attention. If our minds can't get a quick grip on the picture, we have to work a bit harder and look at it for a bit longer – which is good news for the artist.

see for yourself

Draw a golden rectangle, then divide it into thirds in both directions. Now draw a picture using the rule of thirds and the rule of odd numbers and sketching in vanishing points for perspective. How does your picture look?

The vanishing point in this painting by the Italian artist Raphael is between the two central figures – the Greek philosophers Aristotle and Plato. This draws your eye to them.

HOW TO FIND GOLD

If you hold a feather pillow in one hand and a block of concrete the same size in the other... oh, but you can't! The concrete is too heavy. Size and weight don't go together, and that's very useful if you want to test whether or not something is gold.

EUREKA!

About 2,200 years ago, King Hiero II of Syracuse employed a craftsman to make him a crown from a lump of gold that he had weighed. When the man brought back the crown, the king tested it and found that it weighed the same as the lump of gold. But he was still unsure that the craftsman was honest, so he asked the mathematician Archimedes to test the crown. At first, Archimedes could not see how to do this. The story goes that the answer came to him when he watched the water level rise as he got into his bath. Spotting this, he yelled 'Eureka!', which is Greek for 'I've got it!'

A CON DISCOVERED

Archimedes took a lump of gold and a lump of silver, each weighing the same as the crown. The silver lump was bigger because silver is less dense. Density is a measure of how heavy something is for its volume. He dropped each lump into a tub of water and measured how much water escaped from the tub. This was the volume of water displaced. The silver displaced more water because it was bigger. He then put the crown into the tub and measured the water that it displaced.

It was more than the gold and less than the silver, so he knew that the dishonest craftsman had kept some of the gold the king gave him and mixed the rest with silver until it was the right weight.

It was very difficult to measure the volume of a shape like a crown — but Archimedes found a method.

WHY YOU CAN'T DROWN A WITCH

You can use displacement only to measure the volume of something that sinks in water. Something that floats doesn't go completely underwater (obviously, or it would be sinking) so it can't displace its whole volume. It does displace its own weight in water, though. An ancient method of testing an accused witch was to throw her in water. If she sank, she was considered innocent (but drowned). If she floated, she was a witch. This means it would have been impossible to find the volume of a real witch.

19 HOW TO MAKE AN IMPOSSIBLE SHAPE

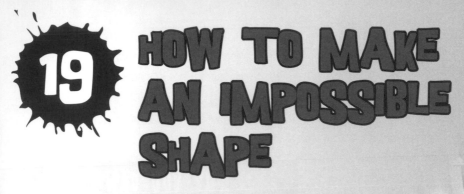

Can a three-dimensional shape have only one side? Can a bottle have an inside that is also its outside, or staircases go at different angles? Some seemingly impossible shapes can actually be made, but others are only ever a trick.

GOING NOWHERE

Take a look at the picture of the staircases on the right. If you imagined people on the stairs, they could all go up and down each staircase quite easily. But what would happen if you took this photograph and built the staircases for people to use?

The staircases would look as pretty as they do in the picture, but they would be completely useless! No one would be able to use the sideways stairs without falling off. Although the staircases work as a two-dimensional objects on paper, in reality in three dimensions, they do not work at all.

☞ *These stairs may look pretty but you wouldn't get very far if you had to climb them!*

ANOTHER DIMENSION?

We live in a world of three physical dimensions. At least, there are three that we deal with every day, though some mathematicians think there are a lot more dimensions we don't usually notice! A single point occupies no dimensions. A line exists in one dimension – it has length but an ideal line has no thickness. A plane exists in two dimensions. Think of an infinitely thin piece of paper – it has an area, but no thickness. A solid shape exists in three dimensions. Everything we encounter in real life exists in three dimensions.

Point   *Line*

Plane

Solid

POSSIBLE IMPOSSIBLES: A NEVERENDING STRIP

A piece of paper is pretty close to being two-dimensional. It has area, but it is very thin. It's quite easy to see that a piece of paper has two sides. We can ignore the thickness as it's so small. Yet it is possible to make a piece of paper into a shape which seems to have only one side. This is called a Möbius strip.

To do this, you need a long strip of paper. You can cut an ordinary sheet in half and tape the two pieces together at one end. Now twist the strip once and tape the other two ends together. Run your finger over the surface of the strip and you will find that you get back to where you started, having covered the whole surface. If you still don't believe it, draw a line with a pencil over the whole surface – you don't need to lift the pencil off the paper to do this. What happens if you cut the Möbius strip in half lengthways?

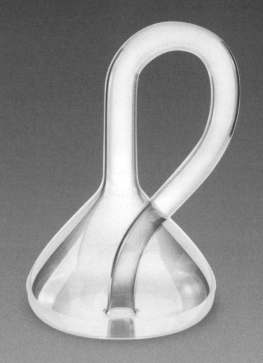

A BOTTLE OF NOTHING

A Möbius strip is a two-dimensional loop with only one side – can we do the same in three dimensions? It's not as easy, but it is possible. A Klein bottle, like the one above, is a glass bottle that exists in three dimensions but is strangely made so that the outside surface is continuous with the inside. It achieves this by having a tube that passes through the outside of the bottle and widens into the opening.

If you were to turn it over and pour water into the opening, the water would, in fact, fill up... from the other end.

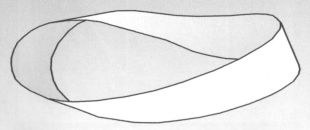

This impossible triangle is an optical illusion; it can be drawn but never made.

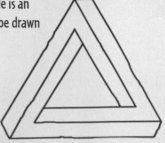

Here's another. How can the parts of the triangle be rearranged to give the lower shape, which has a hole in it?

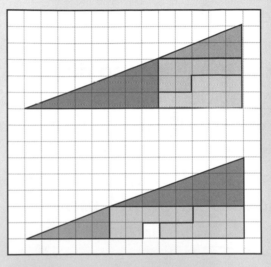

This one is apparently a fork with three prongs – but look more closely.

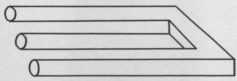

Tricks like this use the spaces in a picture to fool you into seeing shapes.

A common type of optical illusion is one that shows two pictures in one. As soon as you have seen both, it's impossible to decide which thing the picture really shows. It flashes between the two images as you look at it.

If you look very carefully at the pictures above you will see that in the top picture the long sides of the triangles are not actually straight but curve inwards. In the lower picture, they curve outwards. So it's a cheat – the shapes in the top and bottom pictures are not actually the same and the difference is enough to make the blank square.

20 HOW TO SOLVE A CRIME

Years ago, getting away with a crime was a matter of leaving the scene quickly and dumping the evidence. Anyone who did that stood a good chance of escaping punishment. But mathematics and science have changed all that.

WHO ARE YOU?

If you look closely at your fingertips, you will see a pattern of ridges that form your fingerprints. No two people have exactly the same fingerprints – not even identical twins. This means that fingerprints can be used to identify people. You might be able to log onto your laptop using your fingertip, or pay for your school meals by putting your finger on a scanner. Fingerprints never change. As your fingers grow, the prints stay in proportion. Only serious burns or removal of all the skin can get rid of them.

Natural oils from your fingers leave fingerprints on anything you touch.

IN THE LOOP

There are three basic patterns in fingerprints: loops, arches and whorls. Loops account for 60–65 per cent of all fingerprints, whorls for 30–35 per cent and arches for 5 per cent. There are sub-types of these groups that experts can tell apart.

Loop *Whorl* *Arch*

THE GLOVES ARE OFF

A bloody fingerprint was first used to solve a murder in 1892. Today, a forensics expert (someone who uses science to solve crimes) compares fingerprints left at a crime scene with the fingerprints of a suspect. The police keep records of convicted criminals' fingerprints. They compare the prints left at a crime scene with the stored prints to find out whether or not a known criminal might have committed the new crime.

MATCHMAKING

It would take a very long time to compare a new fingerprint with the millions held on record, so the first stage is to cut down the possibilities.

To do this, an expert allocates a number to each finger- and thumb print. Arches and loops are given a 0. Whorls are given a number according to which finger they are on, like this:

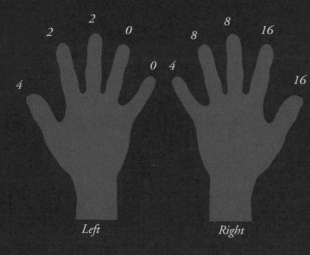

Left   Right

The allocated numbers are then added up in the following way to give two totals:
(Right 1st + Right 3rd + Left thumb + Left 2nd + Left 4th) + 1
and
(Right thumb + Right 2nd + Right 4th + Left 1st + Left 3rd) + 1

The 1 is added to each row so that even if someone had no whorls, there is never a sum that tries to divide into or by zero, which is impossible!

For example, if the right 3rd finger and the left 1st finger had whorls, and the rest were arches or loops, the sums would be:
(0 + 8 + 0 + 0 + 0) + 1 = 9
and
(0 + 0 + 0 + 2 + 0) + 1 = 3
The top number is then divided by the bottom number:
9 ÷ 3 = 3

These prints would need to be compared only with other sets that gave a result of 3. There are 256 possible results, which really cuts down the number of prints to check.

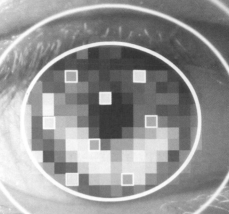

Some security checks use iris scanners, which look at patterns in the eye to identify people.

GENETIC FINGERPRINTS

It's not just your fingertips that are unique. People have toe prints, tongue prints and unique patterns in their eyes – but these are rarely left at the scene of a crime. Criminals often leave tiny traces of their bodies at a crime scene, though – blood, hair, fragments of skin or spit, for example. From these, forensic scientists can collect DNA – the chemical that codes all of the genetic information in our bodies. Everyone's DNA is slightly different so, just like a fingerprint, it can be used to identify someone. The chances of two people having the same DNA are almost zero. DNA testing checks only a portion of the DNA molecule, giving a chance of about 1 in 7,000 that a different person could have left a matching sample.

Counting on DNA

DNA is a very long molecule that looks like a twisted ladder. The 'rungs' of the ladder are made up for four different units in a sequence that varies between people. In fact, 99.9 per cent of DNA is the same for everyone – but that last 0.1 per cent is enough to make us unique. Only identical twins have the same DNA.

By comparing the sequences in particular areas of the DNA, scientists can see whether samples of body tissue left at a crime scene match a sample from a suspect.

21 HOW TO KNOW WHERE YOU ARE GOING

People have been getting lost ever since they stepped out of their caves and followed tasty-looking mammoths into unknown territory. But today, with sat nav systems and GPS phones, getting lost is definitely a thing of the past – isn't it?

WHERE AM I?

GPS stands for Global Positioning System – which just means it works out positions on Earth – and sat nav is short for satellite navigation. Both GPS and sat nav work out your position from radio signals sent from satellites in space. If you have a mobile phone that has GPS, or if there is sat nav in your car, you will always be able to find out where you are, and how to get to wherever you want to go.

CIRCLES AND TRIANGLES

GPS devices work using a mathematical method called triangulation. It sounds as though it should be about triangles, but it is actually more about circles. The GPS system has 24 satellites that orbit Earth at a height of 18,000 km (11,185 miles). In fact, the satellites don't go round Earth at all – they keep up with Earth as it rotates, so they stay above the same place.

☞ *This lost cyclist could do with ditching his paper map for sat nav on his mobile phone!*

WHERE EXACTLY?

The signal from each GPS satellite has information coded into it about which satellite it is from and the exact time the signal was sent. The receiver can work out how long it has taken the signal to get from the satellite. The signals travel at the speed of light, so it takes about 0.06 seconds for the satellite signal to reach Earth, and very tiny variations in this time are used to locate the satellite. From the time taken and the speed, the receiver calculates how far away the satellite is. The receiver works out a circle on Earth of all positions exactly the right distance from the satellite. By taking readings from three or four satellites, the receiver can pinpoint its exact position, which is where all the circles meet.

Each satellite beams radio waves to Earth that can be picked up in a circular patch under the satellite by GPS devices. The circles covered by the satellites overlap, and between them, they cover the whole surface of Earth. Phones or sat nav systems can usually get a signal from three or four satellites and from these, they work out where you are.

FROM HERE TO THERE

GPS is good for finding out where you are, but people usually use sat nav to tell them how to get somewhere. A sat nav system compares your position with a stored computerized map to work out directions. If you take a wrong turn, the sat nav knows because it is always checking your position. It recalculates the route and tells you how to get back on track.

WHERE DID THE MAP COME FROM?

It's all very well to say the sat nav works out how to get you to where you are going by comparing your location with a map, but that map had to be made in the first place.

People began making detailed, accurate maps in the 16th century. The method for measuring distances to places that are hard to get to was – again – triangulation.

Mathematicians can work out the length of the sides of a triangle if they know the length of one side and two angles of the triangle.

see for yourself

You'll need two friends and some chalk for this. Go outside, somewhere you can draw on the ground without being in trouble. You are each a satellite. Stand in a triangle so that you are about arm's length from each other. Now each crouch down and draw a circle around yourself with the chalk. There should be a point or area where all three circles cross. This is where ants with GPS systems would get signals from all three satellites.

So two people at different places on the shore could calculate the distance to an island, for instance. They need to know the distance between the two people, which is easy to measure. Then they each measure the angle of their line of sight to the island in relation to an imaginary line linking the two observers. From this, they can work out the distance to the island.

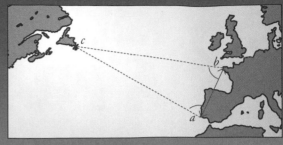

Using triangulation it is possible to work out the distance to point c if the two angles of the triangle at points a and b are known, as well as the distance between point a and point b.

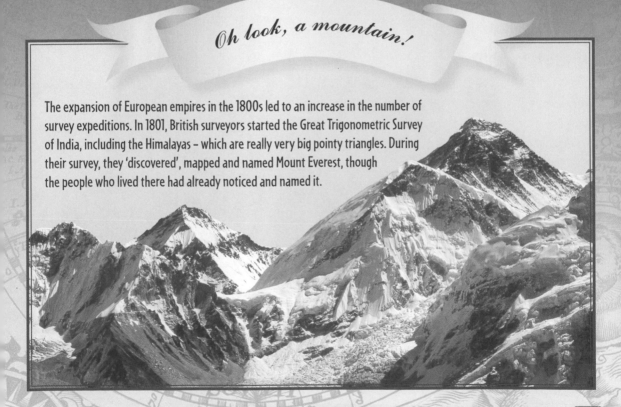

Oh look, a mountain!

The expansion of European empires in the 1800s led to an increase in the number of survey expeditions. In 1801, British surveyors started the Great Trigonometric Survey of India, including the Himalayas – which are really very big pointy triangles. During their survey, they 'discovered', mapped and named Mount Everest, though the people who lived there had already noticed and named it.

22 HOW TO BE A PIRATE

Got your parrot, sword and ship? Good – now you need to learn to read maps, navigate by the Sun and stars, and use a compass. Being a pirate is not all play and plunder!

WHICH WAY?

Pirates did not use large cruise ships with electric lights and GPS navigation systems. For them, the only way of navigating was by the Sun in the day and the Moon and stars at night. They used a compass and a few other basic instruments. Maps are fine near the coast, but out in the open sea there are no landmarks and it's all down to angles. A pirate who was no good with numbers would never make it to the treasure island.

 Treasure chests would stay buried if pirates were not able to read maps.

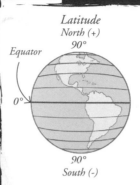

Latitude
North (+)
90°
Equator
0°
90°
South (-)

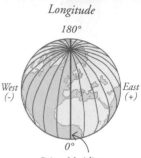

Longitude
180°
West (-)
East (+)
0°
Prime Meridian

Maps and globes show lines that go around Earth. The lines make a grid that forms a reference system for positions. Lines that go around Earth, parallel to the Equator, give latitude. Latitude is measured as the number of degrees from the Equator. Imagine a line drawn from the centre of Earth to a point on the Equator, and then another line from the centre of Earth to a different position. The angle between the two lines gives the latitude of the second position. The latitude of the Equator is 0°. The North Pole has a latitude of 90°N or +90° and the South Pole has a latitude of 90° S or -90°.

Lines that go from the North Pole to the South Pole are used to measure longitude. A line running through Greenwich in London, UK, called the Prime Meridian, is used to measure longitude. It is at 0°. The angle between a line from the centre of Earth to the Prime Meridian and a line from the centre of Earth to the second position gives the longitude. Any position can be given exactly as degrees of latitude and longitude.

STARS AND STICKS

Since ancient times, sailors and pirates have found their way by using the stars. They relied on the North Star in the northern hemisphere because it is always visible. Sailing towards the North Star meant the ship headed north; keeping it to the left meant the ship headed east. But this is vague and sailors soon found the need for something more precise.

They worked out the latitude of their position by measuring the height of the Sun or North Star as an angle from their eye. To take this measurement, they used a cross-staff.

This was a stick, marked with degrees and with a moveable crossbar. The pirate lined up the bottom of the crossbar with the horizon and moved the bar until he could see the appropriate star or Sun at the top of the crossbar. He then read off the angle from the rule. In the northern hemisphere the angle to the North Star is the latitude.

☞ *A sextant and compass enabled a pirate to measure angles and so find his position.*

PIRATE PROGRESS

Later pirates used a sextant. The principle was the same – measuring angles from the horizon to things in the sky – but the method was more accurate. A sextant could be turned sideways and used to measure the angle between the Moon and the North Star. Looking up the angle in a book of tables meant the pirate could match the angle to the corresponding time in London, and from that calculate longitude as well as latitude.

LAND HO!

Once the pirate had found his location, he worked out which way to sail using a map and a compass. The needle of a compass always points to magnetic north, so the pirate needed to calculate the angle between a line drawn to his destination and a line drawn due north.

The compass starts at north (0°) and goes clockwise, so that due east is 90°.

Pieces of eight

Although it sounds mathematical, 'pieces of eight' are nothing to do with numbers. Instead they are pirates' treasure. Pieces of eight were silver Spanish dollars, and the name comes from their value – eight Spanish 'reales'. The US dollar was based on the Spanish dollar, and pieces of eight could be used in the USA until 1857. Pirates who preferred gold searched for gold doubloons, which were worth four pieces of eight.

When the captain told his crew to 'plot a course for 23° east', this meant the ship must point 23° going clockwise from north.

23 HOW TO FLATTEN A PLANET

People have known that Earth is round for at least 2,500 years. But its roundness presents a problem: how do we show the round globe on a flat map?

A GLOBE FOR YOUR POCKET

The best model of the world to show where places are and plan routes between them is a globe. But a globe is not very easy to carry around, and it is not easy to measure distances across it. The obvious answer is to make a flat map that copies the globe. But that is not easy either. If you try to wrap up a ball as a present, you will quickly see just how difficult it is to match the surface of a sphere to a flat piece of paper.

☞ *It would be hard to put this globe in your pocket when you went on a trip!*

TUBES AND CONES

Although it is impossible to wrap a rectangle snugly around a ball, many maps are rectangular in shape. A rolled rectangle makes a cylinder, or tube. Another way to make an accurate map is to show, or project, it onto a cone of paper. Maps of the world are often projections onto a cylinder, cone or flat plane, but they can never show the world as it really is.

THE WORLD'S NOT LIKE THAT!

When we measure a distance over a sphere, we are actually measuring an arc (curved line) in three dimensions. A line drawn all around the globe is a circle. Any line across the surface of the globe is part of a circle. If we flatten a globe to make a map, the curvature is lost and the distance is changed – we are now measuring a flat line in two dimensions.

Cartographers, or map-makers, must choose which features of Earth to represent accurately and which ones to distort or change. Some of the things it is possible to distort are shape, area, direction, distance and scale. The scale is the ratio of the distance on a map to the distance on the ground.

NOT ALL WORLDS ARE ROUND

The different ways of making maps have been developed with Earth in mind, working on the basis that it's a sphere (though in fact it's a slightly squashed sphere). The same methods are used to make maps of other spherical and near-spherical bodies, such as the Moon and Mars. But some of the things whizzing around space are very far from being spherical. The asteroid Ida looks like a potato, more than twice as long as it is wide, and Saturn's moon Hyperion is irregular and sponge-like. These will present new problems to space-travelling map-makers of the future.

DISTORTED MAPS

Some of the ideas we have about the world are the result of distorted maps. On maps made by the Belgian cartographer Gerardus Mercator, Greenland looks as big as the entire continent of South America and much larger than Australia. But Greenland is actually only slightly bigger than Mexico and one-third of the size of Australia!

UP AND DOWN

Being spherical is not the only challenge the world presents to map-makers. It has an uneven surface, with mountains and deep valleys, rolling hills and flat plains. Maps have to find a way of showing how land goes up and down. Imagine a photo of a mountain, taken from above. The pointiness of the mountain is not obvious. The same is true of a map that is a flat plan of an area. If you were planning a walk, you might pick a route that looks like a stroll, but then find it was a difficult climb up a mountain.

Cartographers use contour lines (like the ones in the background opposite) to show how land goes up and down. These wiggly lines show the height above sea level. Each contour line relates to a height. Where the contour lines are close together, there is a steep gradient because the height is changing quickly.

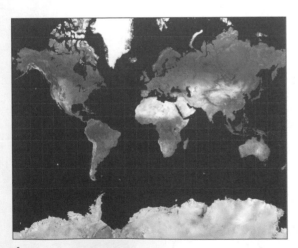

The Mercator projection distorts sizes near the poles, so Greenland looks bigger than it is.

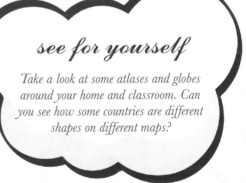

Weird and wonderful maps

Not all maps show the shape and size of an area. Some aim to show something very different, such as political or social information. In these maps, the size of a region is not related to the area of the land or distance between places – but to other data, such as population, wealth or disease levels. This map shows overcrowded houses around the world.

The countries that appear the biggest on this map, are those where there is the most overcrowding in houses. You can see from the map that the USA, Canada and many European countries have very little overcrowding, while countries in Asia, such as India, and Africa, such as Nigeria, have the most overcrowding.

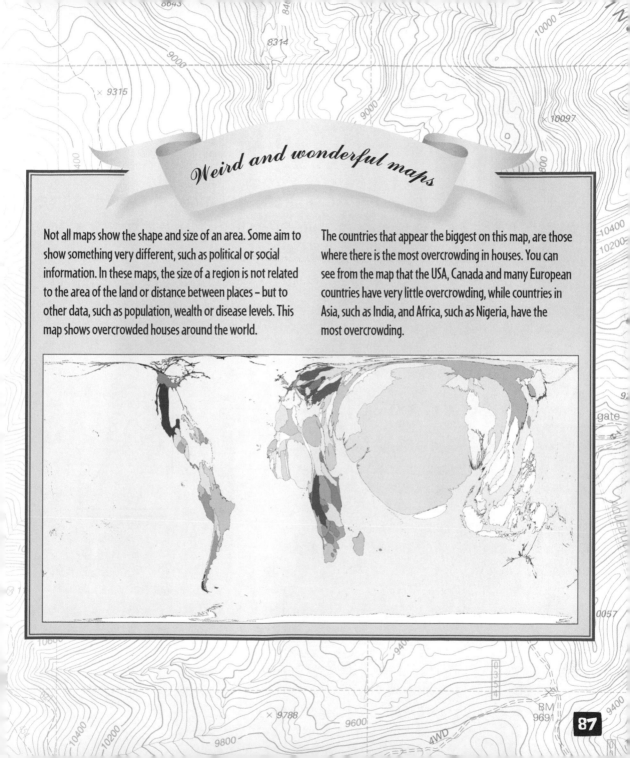

24 HOW TO SLIDE DOWN A SKYSCRAPER

The world's bravest stuntman is attempting a death slide from the top of the world's tallest building. But he doesn't know how much wire he'll need to perform his death-defying trick. Luckily, triangles can save him from going splat on the sidewalk!

SKYSCRAPERS AND TRIANGLES

Triangles are a really useful shape. Our courageous stuntman can work out just how much wire he needs by imagining the skyscraper as one side of a very large triangle. All he then has to do is to measure the height of the building he wants to slide from as well as the distance he wants to land away from the base of that building. He can then use a clever formula developed by Pythagoras (see box opposite).

As he's decided to slide off the world's tallest building, Burj Khalifa in Dubai, UAE, someone has helpfully measured its

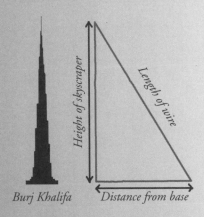

Burj Khalifa — *Height of skyscraper* — *Length of wire* — *Distance from base*

height for him. It is 828 m (2,717 ft) tall, and our stuntman has decided that he wants to land 500 m (1,640 ft) from the base of the skyscraper.

He can then use Pythagoras's method to find out how much wire he needs:

PYTHAGORAS'S THEOREM

Pythagoras was an ancient Greek mathematician. His theorem can be explained like this:

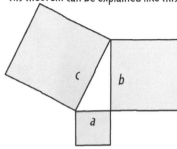

The square of the two short sides added together is equal to the square of the long side (called the hypotenuse). The 'square' means you have to multiply the length by itself.

So $(a^2) + (b^2) = (c^2)$.

Once you have c^2, you need to take the square root of the number to get c. You can do this on a calculator using the $\sqrt{}$ button.

☞ More wire will produce a shallower slide and less will make the drop steeper – either way, it will be pretty exciting.

(height of skyscraper) x (height of skyscraper)
+ (distance from base) x (distance from base)
= (length of wire) x (length of wire)
Adding the measurements makes:

(828 x 828) + (500 x 500) = 935,584

The stuntman needs to find out what number multiplied by itself (or squared) makes 935,584. This number is called the square root. The square root of 935,584 is 967.3, and this is how many metres of wire he needs.

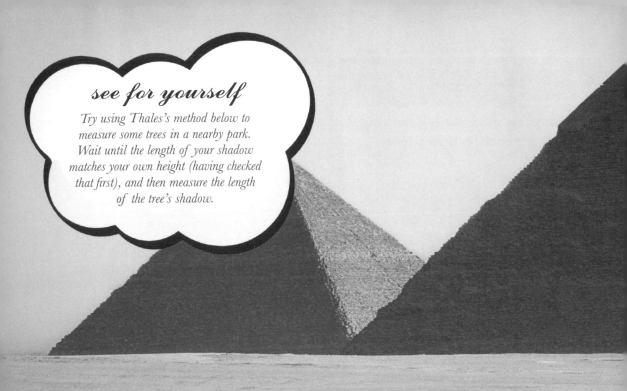

see for yourself

Try using Thales's method below to measure some trees in a nearby park. Wait until the length of your shadow matches your own height (having checked that first), and then measure the length of the tree's shadow.

MEASURING THE PYRAMIDS

Triangles are used to measure distances in lots of ways. The Greek mathematician Thales is said to have worked out the height of the pyramids in Egypt by measuring their shadows. He waited until the Sun was directly overhead and his own shadow was equal to his height, then he measured the length of the pyramids' shadows.

HOW FAT IS EARTH?

Earth is massive, and it's difficult to stand far enough away from it to measure it using triangles. But another Greek

mathematician, called Eratosthenes worked out a way of doing it. Again, he used shadows cast by the Sun.

Eratosthenes knew that when the Sun was directly overhead (at the zenith, or at 90° to the ground) in a town called Syene in southern Egypt, it was 7° off the zenith in his hometown of Alexandria. He assumed the Sun was so far away that he could treat its beams as parallel. He concluded that the distance between Alexandria and Syene must be $7/360$ of the total distance around Earth. Eratosthenes calculated the distance between Syene and Alexandria as 5,000 stadia – one stadia was between 185 m (607 ft) and 192 m (630 ft).

From this, Eratosthenes calculated that each degree of Earth was roughly 700 stadia and so the circumference of Earth must be 700 x 360 = 252,000 stadia. This would give a distance between 46, 620 km (28,968 miles) and 48, 384 km (30, 064 miles), depending on the stadia used. The circumference of Earth is actually 40,008 km (24,860 miles), so his estimate was really not too bad.

Measuring the Moon

You can estimate the size of the Moon during a lunar eclipse. A lunar eclipse happens when Earth's shadow falls over the Moon. When Earth is close enough to the Moon, its shadow is nearly the same size as Earth. When this shadow falls over part of the Moon, it forms an arc (part of a circle). By drawing the whole circle from the arc, we can draw Earth to the same scale as the Moon.

Knowing the size of Earth, we can work out the size of the Moon.

$$ratio = \frac{\text{Moon's image diameter (cm)}}{\text{Earth's shadow diameter (cm)}}$$

So:

Moon's diameter (km) = ratio x Earth's diameter (km)

HOW TO BLOW THINGS UP

How can you fit a dinosaur into your bedroom or turn over a head louse in your hands? The answer is simple: by using a model. A model or drawing, made to scale, uses the same proportions as the real thing but shows it larger or smaller.

SCALING THE HEIGHTS!

When architects want to make a new building, they don't just collect a lot of stone and start to work. Even the ancient Romans and Egyptians knew that this was not the way to do it. A bridge, pyramid or any other large building takes careful planning.

Drawings and models help architects to work out how to put a building together and to show other people how it will look. They need to be very careful that the structure will actually work – that the roof won't fall in and crush people, and that walls will meet at the corners. All this is worked out by making a small version of the structure – a scale model.

In a scale model or drawing, all the proportions are the same as in the real thing, but the distances are different. For example, one metre in a building might be shown as one centimetre in a scale

An architect's scale model can help to show how the building will look once it is finished.

SILLY NUMBERS?

Scale is often shown on drawings, maps or models as a ratio, like this;

1:500

This means that 1 cm or 1 inch on the diagram represents 500 cm or 500 inches in real life.

On old maps, the scale is sometimes shown with units rather than as a ratio, such as 1 inch = 1 mile – every inch on the map is a mile in the real world. It's not shown as a scale because the numbers would look awful – 1:63, 360 as there are 63, 360 inches in a mile.

You may see a line on a map marked with distances, like this:

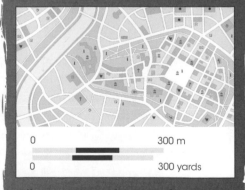

| 0 | 300 m |
| 0 | 300 yards |

You can measure a distance on the map and work out how many metres, kilometres, yards or miles it is in the real world.

model or drawing. This is called a scale of 1:100 (1 centimetre = 100 centimetres). A builder working from the scale plan would need to multiply the numbers on the plan by the scale to find the real size to use.

FINDING YOUR WAY

A map cannot show things at their real size, or it would be as big as the area it shows! Maps are scale drawings of places. The easiest way to see how a map relates to the real world is to look at a satellite photo (taken from space), then switch to a map view of the same area. The distances are the same in the photo and the map, and the map shows the same roads and buildings. The map does not show things that are moving (cars and people), things that might not last very long (bushes) or little details (gates and signposts).

LARGER THAN LIFE

We can scale things up as well as down. This is useful for studying very small things, such as tiny animals, or for designing

Painting a wall

Imagine that you want to paint a mural on your bedroom wall (don't do it without asking!). You could plan it by drawing it on a piece of paper first, and copying it onto the wall, making it larger. Unless your mural is all straight lines and geometric shapes, it will not be easy to do this by measuring and scaling up each line. But there is an easy way to do it. Draw a grid over your small drawing, then draw a larger grid in pencil over the wall. Now you can copy the lines within each small square on the paper into the equivalent big square on the wall.

equipment such as computer chips. To write this, the scale is the other way round – 100:1, for example. This would show something that is 1 millimetre across as 10 centimetres across.

☞ An aerial view of a town shows a similar plan to a map.

see for yourself

Measure your bedroom and then make a plan of it using a scale. Use a different piece of paper to make simple scale drawings of the things in your room: a rectangle for your bed, for example. Cut them out. You can move them around on your plan to work out different ways to arrange your room.

26 HOW TO MAKE A T-REX

If you find a tiny little bone, how can you tell if it came from a huge dinosaur? It is all to do with scale – with relating the size of a part to the size of the whole thing.

THE TOE BONE'S CONNECTED TO...

When people first found dinosaur bones, they had no idea what they were. The largest animals known were blue whales, but they were in the sea, and the largest land animals were elephants, which are much smaller than the largest dinosaurs.

Iguanodon was one of the first dinosaurs to be found and studied. A few bones and teeth from an Iguanodon were found in 1822 in England, UK, by Mary Mantell. Her husband was a fossil collector.

From just one of these bones, an expert could work out how big the dinosaur was.

When he saw fossilized teeth of a type of lizard called an iguana, he realized the dinosaur's teeth were very similar, but about six times bigger. Assuming that an Iguanodon's teeth relate to its body size in the same way as an iguana's teeth, we can guess that an Iguanodon was about six times the size of an iguana. An adult iguana is 1.4–1.6 m (4.6–5.2 ft) long, so that would make an Iguanodon up to 9.6 m (31.5 ft) long. This is close to the real size of Iguanodon fossils found later; Iguanodon were about 9.3 m (30.5 ft) long.

DINNER IN A DINO DINER

The first full-size models of dinosaurs were made of concrete in 1854 by Benjamin Waterhouse Hawkins. He made a hollow life-size model of an Iguanodon, which was used to host a dinner party in the Natural History Museum, London. The invitations to the dinner were sent out on fake pterodactyl wings! Making life-size models of dinosaurs was possible only because naturalists made calculations about the size and weight of dinosaurs by comparing fossils and living animals.

FLESH AND BONES

It's all very well working out how big a dinosaur skeleton was, but that does not tell us how fat or how heavy it was. We have to look at the structure of the bones, too. A heavy body needs strong bones to support it. A very heavy dinosaur like T-rex needed huge hip and leg bones, but a lightweight dinosaur like a velociraptor could have thinner bones.

BIGGER AND FATTER

If a tailbone from one dinosaur is half the length of a similar tailbone from another dinosaur, it's fair to think that the whole first dinosaur was about half the length of the second. But we have to be careful with the idea of 'size'. When comparing lengths, we are looking at one dimension. Imagine that we had samples of finger skin from two different dinosaurs.

Why won't a whale walk?

When a whale is washed up on a beach, it can't move itself back into the sea – and not just because it has no legs. A whale is just too heavy to move on land. It can move in water, because water supports its weight. On land, it would need very thick legs to support its huge, blubbery body, and then it would need a much stronger skeleton, and then it would weigh even more, so it would need even thicker legs... It's an unsolvable problem; whales are better off in the sea because the mathematics won't work for them to live on land.

The area of finger skin of the first dinosaur (call it dinosaur A) is four times the area of the finger skin of the second dinosaur (dinosaur B). Does that mean dinosaur B was a quarter the size of dinosaur A? That depends on what you mean by size. If you double the length and width of a shape, its area (the length x width) increases by 4 ($2 \times 2 = 4$):

So if dinosaur A has four times the area of dinosaur B, it is only twice as long.

THREE DIMENSIONS

In three dimensions, the dinosaur is even bigger! Doubling each dimension (height, length, width) means the volume of a shape increases by 8 ($2 \times 2 \times 2 = 8$).

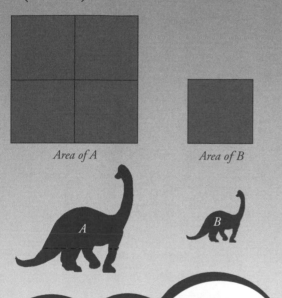

Area of A   *Area of B*

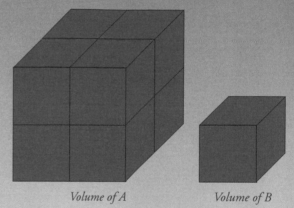

Volume of A   *Volume of B*

So if dinosaur A has a toe bone twice as long as dinosaur B, dinosaur A may be twice as long, but have four times as much skin, and eight times as much body as dinosaur B.

We could test the exact volume of two dinosaurs – if we had them – by dropping each in a large bath and measuring the water that overflowed (just like Archimedes and the golden crown, see pages 66–67).

see for yourself

Use plastic bricks to make identical shapes in different sizes. You can measure their length and area using a ruler, and measure their volume using a measuring jug filled with water. If you make an irregular shape, and double every dimension, does the volume still increase eight times?

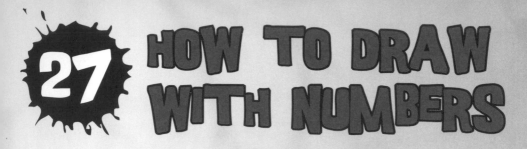

27 HOW TO DRAW WITH NUMBERS

You have probably heard the expression 'a picture is worth a thousand words'. It can also be worth a thousand numbers! It's often easier to get an idea of what numbers show if they are used to make a picture – a graph of some kind – than just shown as a list or table.

I SPY A PIE

A pie chart is a clear and simple type of graph. It's good for showing proportions, such as how many of a group of people like different sports, or what colour hair they have. A pie chart is a circle divided into portions of different sizes that represent the data.

Imagine you live in one of those villages in a forest that you see in scary movies. You have carried out a survey to find out which monster people are most afraid of in the village. Here are the results. It's easy to see from the pie chart on the left of this page that more than half of the people are most scared of vampires.

COLUMNS AND BARS

A pie chart is good when you want to show the proportions of a sample (or group) that fall into different sections, but it doesn't work when there are lots of different categories or values.

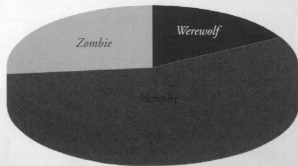

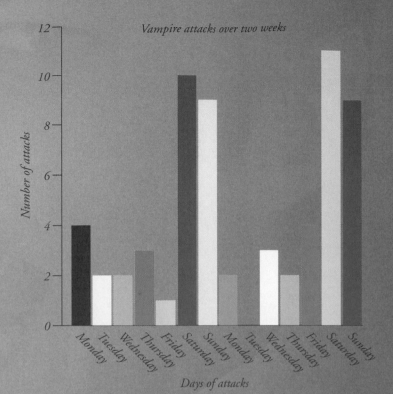

Vampire attacks over two weeks

Number of attacks (y-axis)

Days of attacks (x-axis): Monday, Tuesday, Wednesday, Thursday, Friday, Saturday, Sunday, Monday, Tuesday, Wednesday, Thursday, Friday, Saturday, Sunday

Each side of the bar chart is called an axis, with the x-axis running along the bottom, and the y-axis running up the side.

A bar or column chart is better if you want to show countable values. Now you know that people in the monster village are most scared of vampires, the village leaders have decided to tackle the problem. The local vampire hunter has drawn up a list of vampire attacks over two weeks so that he can plan his strategy. The chart looks like the one above. From the chart, you can see that most vampire attacks happen at the weekend, so that would be a good time for the vampire hunter to go out (and everyone else to stay at home).

ON THE RIGHT LINES

There is a whole number of vampire attacks each day, and they are all on named days – there can't be 3½ attacks, and no attack can happen between Monday and Tuesday. This type of data is good for showing in a bar chart. But if you were plotting something that changes all the time, so that there are values between those you have collected, a line graph would be better.

The vampire hunter has put a thermometer in the earth of the graveyard, because he knows the soil warms up when the vampires start to move. He tracks the temperature over a Saturday afternoon and evening so that he can tell when the vampires are stirring. Here are his results:

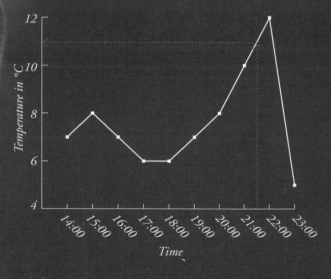

Connecting the points on the graph produces a continuous line.

The graph shows that the temperature rises through the early evening until it is highest at 22:00, then it falls – all the vampires are out of their graves by 23:00. Because a line graph shows a continuous state, we can use the line to get estimated values between the data points.

see for yourself

Carry out a survey of your own, perhaps of what types of pet your friends have, or what time they go to bed, and draw a suitable graph.

If the vampire hunter wanted to know the temperature at 21:30, he could use the graph to find out. He could draw a line up from halfway between 21:00 and 22:00 on the x-axis to meet the line of the graph, then draw a line across to the y-axis (see the dotted red lines) to read off the temperature value of 11 °C (51.8 °F).

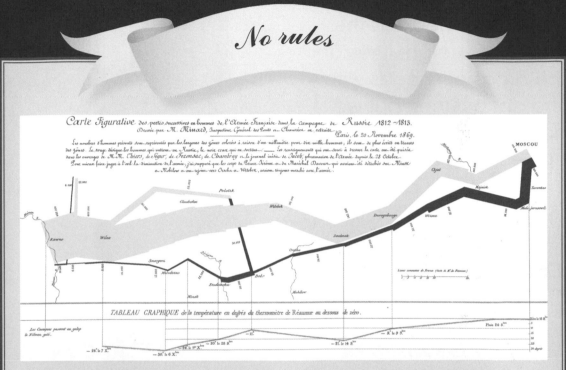

You don't have to stick to pie, bar and line graphs. Some people have come up with unusual ways of showing data in completely new types of graph. One very striking graph shows how many of Napoleon's soldiers died during a disastrous campaign to attack Moscow in 1812. The shape of the line follows the route to Moscow. The thickness of the line shows the size of the army (number of soldiers). It is widest at the start of the journey and gets narrower as men die. By the time it reaches Moscow, the line is much thinner. The return journey is shown in a different colour and is very thin at the end. The difference between the fat line of men who set off and the tiny line of men who returned shows just how few of the soldiers survived.

28

HOW TO SLICE A PIE

It's easy to measure the length of straight lines and the areas of shapes with straight outlines, but we cannot work out the length of curved lines and the area of circles without a very special number called 'pi' (say 'pie').

HOW BIG IS A PI?

People have been trying to work out the area of a circle or the length of a line around a circle, which is called the circumference, for a very long time. Thousands of years ago, they noticed that the ratio (you can read more about ratios on page 62) between the circumference and the diameter (a line drawn through the middle of the circle) is the same for all circles. This means that if you multiply the diameter by a particular number, you always get the circumference.

That number is called pi, so:

circumference = pi x diameter

Pi is shown by the Greek letter π. But pi is not a whole number, a fraction or even a simple decimal. In ancient Babylon (now Iraq), people used 3.125 (3⅛) as their value of pi. They worked it out by drawing a hexagon around a circle and measuring its perimeter (outline). The Greek mathematician Archimedes

You can even use pi to find out just how big a piece of pie is.

Strangely, pi turns up in rivers as well as in circles and spheres. The actual length of a river that winds through the countryside from its source to where it joins the sea is a much longer distance than a straight line drawn between the source of the river and its end. As rivers choose their paths according to the local land, cutting through soft rock, flowing downhill and avoiding mountains and other lumps, you would not expect any pattern in the difference between the straight and winding paths. Astonishingly, though, if you divide the length of the winding path by the length of the straight path, the answer is always very close to pi.

calculated a better value by drawing polygons around the outside and inside of a circle and measuring the two perimeters. This gave him upper and lower limits for the value of pi. By using more and more sides for his polygons, he brought the limits closer together and settled on the value 3½ for pi.

Pi is an irrational number, which means that the digits after the decimal point go on forever. Computers can calculate pi to more than two thousand billion digits, and they still haven't found any pattern in it.

WORKING WITH PI AND PIES

Pi can be used to work out the circumference of a circle, which is the distance around its outside. We can also calculate pi by dividing the circumference by the diameter.

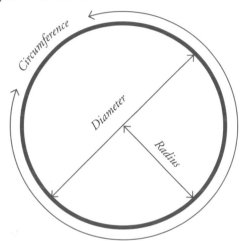

Circumference ÷ Diameter = π = 3.14159...

The radius of a circle (a line drawn from the centre of the circle to the outside) is half its diameter. This means that:

circumference = 2 x radius x pi = 2πr

You can use 3.14 as a rough estimate of pi, or the π button on your calculator.

CROP CIRCLES

Let's try pi out on a puzzle. A farmer wants to make crop circles in his field to try and attract tourists and earn some money.

To do this, he's going to use a length of wood to flatten the wheat, fixing one end to the ground and walking around, pushing down on the wheat to flatten a circle. He knows how long his piece of wood is, but he doesn't want to damage too much of his crop, so he wants to know how big a circle it would make. He can do this by using pi.

The length of the piece of wood will be the radius of the circle, so, if the piece of wood is 3 metres long, he can use the formula:

2 x 3 x π
= 6 x 3.14159... = 18.84954...

So the farmer will create a crop circle with a circumference that's a little over 18.8 metres.

FIND THE AREA

However, the farmer could really do with finding out the area of the crop circle. And pi can help him out here as well. The formula to calculate the area of a circle is

pi x (radius x radius) = πr²

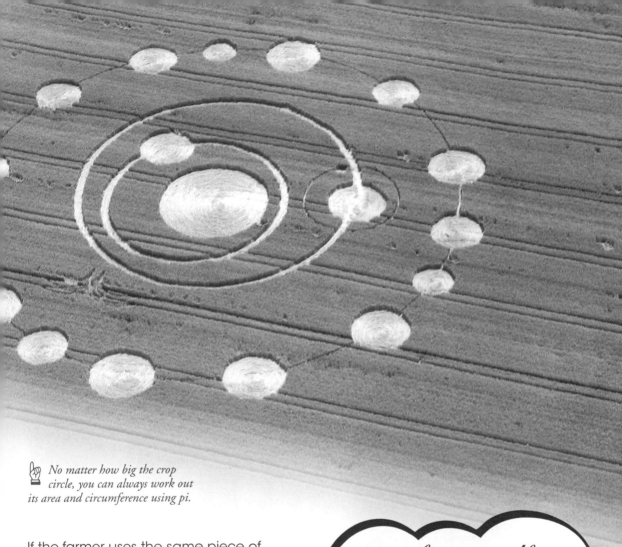

No matter how big the crop circle, you can always work out its area and circumference using pi.

If the farmer uses the same piece of wood, he will create a circle that covers an area of:

3.14159... x (3 x 3) = 3.14159... x 9
= 28.27431...

So any crop circle the farmer makes with that piece of wood will cover an area of nearly 28.3 m² (metres squared).

see for yourself

Celebrate pi day! Pi day is on March 14, because the date can be written 3.14. You could celebrate by making crop circles in the grass in a nearby park or by making cakes and pies with a π symbol.

29

HOW TO GET OUT OF JAIL FREE

Most games are competitive – you want to win, and that means your competitors must lose. But sometimes working with others rather than against them can be to your advantage.

THE PRISONERS' DILEMMA

Two people have been arrested for robbing a bank. They are in different cells and cannot talk to each other. They are each offered a deal.

If one confesses and the other stays silent, the one who confesses will be set free and the other will spend ten years in prison. If both confess, they will both go to prison for two years. If both stay silent, the court will not have the evidence to convict either

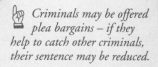

Criminals may be offered plea bargains – if they help to catch other criminals, their sentence may be reduced.

		Prisoner B	
		Confess	Stay silent
Prisoner A	Confess	**A** 2 years **B** 2 years	**A** 0 years **B** 10 years
	Stay silent	**A** 10 years **B** 0 years	**A** 1 year **B** 1 year

of them of a serious crime, so they will go to prison for only one year. What should the prisoners do?

This might seem to have nothing at all to do with mathematics, but it is part of something called 'game theory'. How games are played and their outcomes often depend on mathematics.

The worst thing that can happen is if one prisoner stays silent and the other confesses – but the best outcome for both is if they both stay silent.

NOT ENOUGH FISH

Fishing boats around the world have taken too many fish from the sea, so now some fish are in danger of dying out. Fishermen have made agreements to take only a certain number of fish each year. This agreement means that each fisherman will be poorer, but the fish will survive so that they can carry on fishing in the future. If some fishermen broke the agreement, the others would lose out. If they all broke the agreement, the fish would all be taken and everyone would lose out eventually.

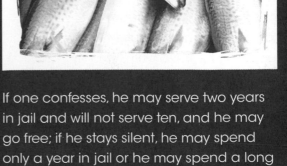

If one confesses, he may serve two years in jail and will not serve ten, and he may go free; if he stays silent, he may spend only a year in jail or he may spend a long time in jail. What would you do?

WORK TOGETHER OR WORK APART?

The prisoners' dilemma is a one-off situation – the prisoners hopefully won't get into the same mess again if released. But the dilemma is rather different if it is an ongoing situation, when each can learn from the consequences of their choices.

Imagine two ice-cream vans, Chilly Ice and Frosty Cream. Both vans sell ice creams for £1 in the same area. They agree to stick to this price, but Chilly Ice decides to be sneaky and sell ice creams for just 80p around the corner. At the end of the first month, Chilly Ice's profits have gone up by £1,000 and Frosty Cream's have gone down. Frosty Cream becomes suspicious and decides to check up on his competitor. He finds out what Chilly Ice has done. To get back at Chilly Ice, Frosty Cream sells ice creams for 75p. Chilly Ice can't afford to sell his ice cream for less than 75p, so suffers because he cheated.

From this, Chilly Ice might learn not to cheat next time – it will depend on how much he loses

overall as a result of cheating. Although the ice-cream sellers lose out, the customers win as they all get cheaper ice cream.

Sometimes, competing businesses might go on dropping their prices further until they cannot afford to do it any more. In the end, they usually reach some type of agreement as intense competition is too damaging to both of them.

FORMING ALLIANCES

Just as the prisoners and ice-cream sellers needed to work together to get the best result, some small countries form friendly alliances with their neighbours. These alliances mean that the small countries can trade with each other and they do not have to worry as much about their larger neighbours attacking them. By joining forces they can be more effective in trade and war.

CHILLY ICE
Ice cream £1 now 80p

Male animals, such as deer, compete for mates. Some males fight viciously, but not many kill each other in these fights. Although it is to the winner's advantage to kill a rival in case he comes back later, if this actually happens, the whole group of animals will suffer. Eventually, so many males will have died in fights that there will not be enough left for the animals to breed and they will die out.

To solve this problem, nature favours a cooperative strategy – the animals fight, but the loser gives up before he is killed. He may later fight a weaker male and win, and he would still get to mate because he isn't dead!

30

HOW TO SEE AROUND EARTH

Have you noticed how, as you grow taller, you can see farther? You can see onto higher shelves, see what is on the table and see over walls. It would work even better if you could grow to be a huge giant.

GROW UP!

Why can you see farther if you go higher up? Well, most obviously, there are fewer things in the way. If you lie on the floor, lots of things block your view. Just think, if you were a worm, you would be able to see only a few metres ahead – or you would if worms had eyes. But there's more to it than just being able to see over obstacles. If you go up a mountain, or a very tall building, you can see over all the obstacles – but you still can't see for ever. You could never see the other side of the world, however high

see for yourself

Next time you are near a hill with a clear view of the horizon, try this out. Watch the Sun set from the bottom of the hill. Then run up the hill as fast as you can. If you are quick enough, you will be able to watch the sunset again from farther up the hill!

you were – even if you were in space. You can only ever see as far as the horizon – the boundary between land and sky.

Many of the skyscrapers in New York City, USA, have observation decks where you can stand to have a view over the whole city.

HOW FAR TO THE HORIZON?

There is a mathematical relationship between how high up you are and how far you can see. If you are 2 m (7 ft) up you can see for 5 km (3 miles) if there is nothing in the way. If you go up a 200-m (660-ft) tower, you can see for nearly 50 km (30 miles).

You can find the distance to the horizon in kilometres by multiplying the square root of your height above the ground in metres by 3.5.

$$(\sqrt{\text{height above the ground}}) \times 3.5 = \text{distance to the horizon}$$

So if you are 100 metres up , the distance to the horizon can be worked out as:

$$(\sqrt{100}) \times 3.5 = 35 \text{ km}.$$

If you kept going higher, the world would start to curve away from you. From a spaceship really high up over the North Pole, you still could not see beyond the Equator.

Because Earth is a very big sphere, there will always be a limit to how far you can see.

OVER THE HORIZON

The reason that ships disappear from view is not because they sail off the edge of Earth, but because Earth is a sphere.

Old sailing ships had a look-out post high on the main mast, called the crow's nest. A sailor in the crow's nest could see farther than a sailor on the deck and so was the first to see land – or approaching pirates. The horizon was farther away from the crow's nest, but it was still there.

WHICH PLANET ARE YOU ON?

The distance to the horizon depends on the curvature of the planet on which you are standing. If you were on a different planet from Earth, you would see a greater or lesser distance to the horizon, depending on the planet. For example, if you could stand on Neptune (which you can't because it is made of gas) you could see much farther because it is a lot larger than Earth.

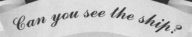

If you stand on the beach and look out to sea, sooner or later you will see a ship approaching. As a ship comes over the horizon, you see its mast or funnel first, and then the lower part of the ship comes into view. Even if you use a telescope, you can't see the lower part of the ship to start with. That's because the curvature of Earth means the lowest part of the ship is still hidden behind the curve of Earth.

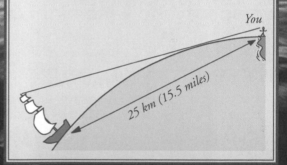

You

25 km (15.5 miles)

If you stood on Earth's Moon, the distance would be different again. Because the Moon is smaller than Earth, it curves away more quickly and so you would not be able to see as far.

DON'T BELIEVE THE HYPE

We all know now that Earth is a sphere, but throughout the ages, some people believed that it was flat instead. While there isn't really any excuse for this if you live near the sea and can watch ships

and boats coming and going, it is a little more excusable if you live inland.

The Mayan people, who lived in South America more than 1,000 years ago, believed that Earth was flat and square. They also believed that at each corner, there was a jaguar of a different colour: red in the east; white in the north; black in the west and yellow in the south. They believed that these four jaguars held up the sky.

31 HOW TO COUNT LIKE A ROMAN

Our numbering system is very efficient: we can write any number up to 99 using only two digits. The Romans were not so lucky. A Roman aged 88 would have to write eight digits to give his age.

LETTERS FOR NUMBERS

Our numerals came from the Arab world less than a thousand years ago. Before that, we used the system that the Romans used. Without any special squiggles to write as numbers, they just used letters, repeating and rearranging them as needed (see below). They probably chose L, X, V and I as their main numerals because they are made up of straight lines and so are easy to carve into stone. Originally, they used IIII for four but later switched to IV, which meant 'one before five'. They did the same for nine (IX – one before ten) and for 40 (XL – ten before 50) and so on.

I = 1   V = 5   X = 10   L = 50   C = 100
D = 500   M = 1000

XIX = 19   XXXII = 32   LI = 51   LXVII = 67
XCIX = 99   MDCLXXVI =1,676   MMXII = 2,012

HARD SUMS

It is very difficult to do sums with Roman numerals, and that's why our current number system took over. Look what happens with even the simplest sum:

XIV
+ XXXI
———
XLV

In our number system, the position of a digit shows its value. A digit on its own means that many units; a two-digit number shows how many tens and how many units. This system makes sums written out like this easy to do as we can just add up the numbers in each column:

14
+ 31
———
45

If two numbers add up to more than ten, then we simply add the extra digits to the next column along.

MODERN-DAY ROMANS

You can still see Roman numerals used today. Films and TV shows often give the year they were made in Roman numerals – such as MMXI for 2011. The most likely place to spot Roman numerals is on a clock face.

Many clocks show '4' as 'IIII' because it balances better than 'IV' with 'VIII' (8) on the other side.

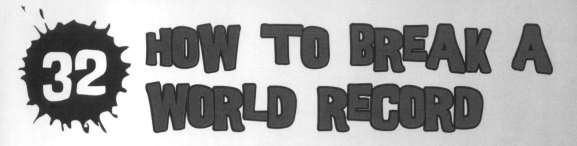

32 HOW TO BREAK A WORLD RECORD

When the ancient Greeks started the Olympic Games more than 2,000 years ago, they just watched the finish line to see who won a race. Today, high-tech equipment is used to measure the times and distances in sporting events. And just winning isn't enough – great athletes want to break world records and that takes split-second timing.

HOW FAST IS FAST?

As athletes have become faster and faster, world records have become even harder to beat. Today, fractions of a second are vital in separating very good athletes from the very best. A hundred years ago, runners were timed using a stopwatch.

Decimals are shown by numbers after a decimal point. The first figure after the decimal point shows the number of tenths, the next figure shows hundredths and the next thousandths, and so on. So 0.1234 means one tenth, two hundredths, three thousandths and four ten-thousandths. The numbers become smaller as you move away from the decimal point to the right. In just the same way, the numbers get bigger moving away from it to the left.

FRACTIONS

When you have to share your birthday cake between friends, fractions are very important. For seven friends, cutting the cake is easy as you have to divide it into eight (remember you need a slice, too!). Cut it in half once, cut each half in half again to get quarters, and each quarter in half to get eight pieces. It's harder to divide a cake into 11 pieces, so pick your guest list carefully.

DECIMAL IS BETTER

Fractions are all very well for cakes, but they're not as useful for record-breaking race times. We don't have to worry about runners who finish races in nine and thirteen-seventeenths seconds – we use decimals instead. In the future, when runners have shaved their times even further, we may measure their times to microseconds (thousandths of a second).

Today, electronic timers that are accurate to a hundredth of a second are used. The difference between the top two 100-metre sprinters can be less than a tenth of a second. If we weren't able to measure such tiny intervals, we would not be able to say who was the faster runner.

A good start in a race can make the difference between breaking the world record and finishing second.

33 HOW TO COMPARE A FLEA TO AN ELEPHANT

It's useful to be able to measure things, but some things are massive and some are minute, so we can't measure them all in the same way. We need to use different units of measurement for different purposes.

FROM ELBOWS TO MILES

Thousands of years ago, when people first started to measure distances, they used parts of their bodies as the units of measurement. The ancient Egyptians used the distance from a person's elbow to a fingertip. They called it a cubit and divided it into palms and digits, which related to the width of the palm of the hand and the length of a finger. A foot was the length of a person's foot, and a yard was an average pace.

These measurements were fine when people wanted to measure things that could be paced out or measured by hand, but they are not much use for measuring distances between cities or for looking at bacteria under a microscope.

MANY MEASURES

Before metres and grams, many different units of measurement were used. Small items were measured in fractions of an inch, then there were 12 inches to a foot, three feet to a yard and 1,760 yards to a mile.

For tiny measurements, there were three barleycorns to an inch, and four poppy seeds to a barleycorn.

Large things such as elephants need bigger units of measurement.

WHOSE ELBOW?

When measures of length were based on parts of the body, there was plenty of scope for argument because not everyone had the same size forearm, thumb or foot. After a while, people began to use a 'standard' elbow or foot. In ancient Egypt, the cubit was based on the pharaoh's forearm. At least that meant the length of the cubit changed only when one pharaoh died and another took over. A standard cubit rule, made of wood, was used because the pharaoh was not always around when something had to be measured.

It must have been difficult to remember all these different measurements and how they related to each other. The multiples – 3, 4, 10, 22, and 1,760 – made the mathematics of converting between units tricky, too. To make matters worse, the measurements were different sizes (but with the same names) in different places. Luckily in the late 1700s, the metric system of metres and grams was invented to make it all much simpler.

This is what a cat flea looks like under a microscope. It's really only about 0.5 mm (0.02 in) long.

TEN RULES

The metric system comes with a set of prefixes (bits to put in front of words) that are the same for all metric units. The table below has a list of them.

Prefix	Name of unit	Fraction/multiple
pico	picometre	$\frac{1}{1,000,000,000,000}$
nano	nanometre	$\frac{1}{1,000,000,000}$
micro	micrometre	$\frac{1}{1,000,000}$
milli	millimetre	$\frac{1}{1,000}$
centi	centimetre	$\frac{1}{100}$
–	metre	1
kilo	kilometre	1,000

The prefix 'milli' means a thousandth, so a millimeter is a thousandth of a metre and a milligram is a thousandth of a gram. 'Kilo' means 'thousand'. A kilometre is 1,000 metres and a kilogram is 1,000 grams. You could measure a flea in millimetres and milligrams, but you would measure an elephant in metres and kilograms.

The prefix for the smallest unit is yocto. A yoctometre is $1 \div 10^{24}$ of a metre; the largest is a yottametre, or 10^{24} metres. A yoctometre could be used to measure sizes within atoms. An electron is $\frac{1}{100}$ of a yoctometre across. A yottametre can be used to measure distances in space. One yottametre is equivalent to 110 million light years (the distance light can travel in 110 million years). A yottametre is 10^{48} times as big as a yoctometre.

DON'T BE PICKY!

We have to be sensible when choosing how accurately to measure something – there is no point in being too picky. You could not measure your height to the nearest yoctometre even if you wanted to, because atoms move around and whizz off your body all the time so your height is constantly changing if you look too closely. It is good enough to measure your height to a centimetre. But if you were measuring a flea in centimetres you would have to say it was 0 centimetres tall – or not there at all! It would be better to use millimetres.

It won't fit!

If you need to fit one thing inside another, you have to measure more accurately than usual.

If you want to put a bookshelf in your room, but the shelf is longer than the wall by a millimetre, it just won't fit – the walls are not going to move out of the way simply because the difference is not worth bothering with.

see for yourself

Which units would you use to measure these four items:
1. *An ant*
2. *A room*
3. *A mountain*
4. *An international journey?*

34 HOW TO MAKE AN AMAZING MAZE

When you are inside a maze, it seems to be random and confusing, but if you look at a maze from above there is often a pattern to it. There are lots of ways of making your own mazes to amaze your friends.

NOT ALL A JUMBLE

While you can make a maze that is not based on a pattern, there are some basic types of maze. Some have only one route through with no branches or choices – they are really a long walk in a small space. Others have only one correct route. They have branches and choices that can lead you up the wrong path.

Some mazes have more than one path through. You need to choose which type you want to make before you start, as your maze really will be a jumble if you don't know what you are doing.

Some mazes have something in the middle for you to discover when you get there.

THE MINOTAUR!

The Greek legend of the minotaur tells how the hero, Theseus, used a thread to find his way through a labyrinth (maze) in Crete. The labyrinth was the home of a terrible monster, called a minotaur. The minotaur had the head of a bull and the body of man and it ate children! Theseus unwound the thread on his way into the maze and followed it back after he had killed the minotaur. The Cretan maze design was used a lot in Crete and other areas of Greece, but Theseus would not have needed the string to get out of the maze – there is only one path, and it's impossible to get lost!

ONE WAY

A maze with only one route through it is called a unicursal maze. The oldest known unicursal maze design is the Cretan maze, which is more than 3,200 years old. You can draw your own Cretan maze like this: start with a cross, and put four dots between the arms:

Next, join the top of the cross to the top left dot, going around the top right dot.

You need to join all the dots to the arms of the cross, but without ever crossing a line you have drawn. Next, join the top right dot to the right-hand arm of the cross, going round your curved line.

Now join the left arm of the cross to the bottom left dot, going around the bottom right dot and again enclosing all the lines you have drawn so far:

Lastly, join the remaining dot to the bottom of the cross, enclosing all the lines you have drawn so far:

You can make a Cretan maze in other shapes, such as a square. It will look like this:

MAKE A MAZE

To make a maze, draw a grid with an odd number of squares making up each side. Leaving every other square white, shade in a grid. Shade in one square darkly and the other lightly so that you have a pattern like the one below. The outer wall can all be dark, but leave two cells white to be the entrance and two for the exit.

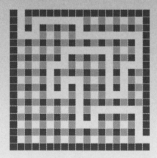

Entrance

Exit

Next, rub out pale cells to make a path through the maze, like this:

Now you have the path planned, colour in or rub out the remaining pale cells to make paths, dead ends and walls.

Shopping mazes

Mazes are not only for fun. Some shops are designed in a way similar to unicursal mazes. They make shoppers follow a confusing zig-zag route through the store so that they see all the products and are more likely to buy things they had not intended buying or looking for.

35 HOW TO CAUSE A STORM

Have you ever thought about how tiny changes can make a huge difference in life? If your mum had had a headache and decided not to go out on the day she met your dad, you might not have been born. The same thing happens in the natural world.

CHAOS AND THE WEATHER

In 1961, Edward Lorenz tried to predict the weather using a computer. He was using figures accurate to six decimal places, but his computer printed out the data to just three decimal places. So if he typed in 0.123456, his computer would print 0.123. Wanting to run one of his calculations again, he tried to save time by typing in the figures from the printout. This meant he was using figures that were only accurate to $1/1000$. This is a tiny amount, so he did not think it would matter, but the predicted weather was completely different using these new figures. What he had discovered became chaos theory.

Chaotic systems are so complicated that they look random, but they are actually very sensitive. Even tiny changes in the starting conditions can make a huge difference to the outcome.

NEVER MIND THE WEATHER

Predicting the weather accurately is extremely difficult because there are so many factors that affect it. Changing any of these conditions, even slightly, has an effect that can become greater and greater. Because there are so many things to take into account, the number of possible results increases very quickly, and any small mistake can lead to a large

Some extreme weather events, such as this twister, are possible to predict only with the most powerful computers.

SEAGULLS AND BUTTERFLIES

One weather scientist suggested that the flap of a seagull's wings could change Earth's weather for ever. Later people swapped the seagull for an even smaller butterfly and suggested it could cause a tornado. The tiny disturbance of the air caused by the moving wings might be enough, sometimes, to have very large knock-on effects. This is sometimes called the 'butterfly effect'. By coincidence, a graph of some types of chaotic behaviour is shaped like butterfly wings.

error in the prediction. Even with very powerful computers, we can predict the weather with confidence only for a few days at a time – and even then, the predictions are sometimes wrong.

Before computers were developed, the calculations involved in predicting the weather were so difficult, and took so long, that the weather couldn't be predicted precisely at all.

HOW CHAOTIC IS CHAOS?

Chaos is a complete lack of order, and chaos theory is not actually chaotic at all. The system is entirely predictable in theory, it's just that it is too difficult – often impossible – to measure the starting conditions accurately enough to predict the outcome. Many 'chaotic' systems have so many variables (conditions that can affect what happens) that we have not come up with calculations that can take account of all of them.

If you put a ball on the very top of a mountain, you could not predict which way it would roll down. It would depend on tiny variations of the ground on each side of the ball, whether you placed it exactly centrally, whether you accidentally gave it even a tiny push in one direction, the direction of the wind, and other factors impossible to measure. Yet if you knew all of the conditions, it would be possible to predict how the ball would roll.

THE DOMINO EFFECT

The domino effect shows how a tiny movement can set off a whole chain of events. Unlike the butterfly effect, the events are predictable. It's called the domino effect because it can be demonstrated by lining up dominoes and knocking over the first one, causing the others to fall down one by one.

The domino effect is a predictable chain of events.

see for yourself

Compare the domino effect and the butterfly effect. To see the domino effect, line up a row of dominoes standing on edge. Push over the first domino and see all the others fall. To see the butterfly effect, take a bowl of beads and throw them up in the air. If you knew enough, you would be able to predict where each would land, but the result looks chaotic.

36 HOW TO BUILD A BRIDGE

Next time you cross a bridge, think about what holds it up. Sometimes you can see pillars that support it. But some bridges seem to stay up on their own.

A PLANK OVER A STREAM

Many thousands of years ago, our distant ancestors would have used the first bridges. These were probably tree trunks laid across a stream. Later, flat planks were put over streams because it is easier to walk across a flat plank than a round tree trunk. This simple type of bridge is called a beam bridge. But how far can you take the design?

Originally it was hard to make a bridge longer than a tree – but even if you used something longer and stronger than a tree trunk, you could not extend it very far. A long bridge, supported only at the ends, would sag in the middle. If it was used as a roadway, it would probably break under heavy traffic.

MAKING STRONGER BRIDGES

One way of making a bridge stronger is to put supports under the middle, but this is not always a very practical solution. If you build a bridge over a river, putting supports in the middle might be difficult to do and the supports could get in the way of boats.

The problem is solved by building an arch. This way, the bridge's own weight keeps it up. An arch bridge does not need extra supports and it does not even need mortar between the bricks. The curve of the bridge is the clue to its strength; the weight of the bridge pushes the stone blocks or bricks together. The closer the arch is to a semicircle, the stronger it will be – and the more room there will be for boats to go underneath.

GETTING SQUASHED AND STRETCHED

A bridge has to cope with two different stresses: compression and tension. Compression squashes the thing it acts on. Tension stretches the thing it acts on.

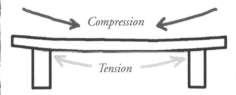

In a beam bridge (like a plank over a stream), compression shortens the top surface and tension stretches the bottom surface of the bridge. The bridge will sag and break if it is not well supported.

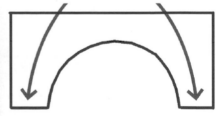

An arch bridge is much more efficient. The compression caused by traffic on the bridge is concentrated at the ends of the bridge, which are supported by the ground. There is very little tension acting on a bridge like this.

TRIANGLES TO THE RESCUE

Triangles are often used in building because they can't be twisted or squashed out of shape. The shape of a triangle cannot be changed without changing the length of one of the sides, so it is an extremely strong support in bridges and buildings. Extra diagonal supports are often added to rectangular shapes to turn them into pairs of triangles.

MORE ARCHES

Cathedrals and other buildings, such as castles, that were built during medieval times have incredibly tall walls. If the ground shifts slightly, pressure from the side could cause these walls to collapse. To stop this from happening, supporting arches called flying buttresses, are used to spread the stress on the building and to strengthen it.

Triangles and squares

Some bridges use triangles to make them stronger. Four-sided shapes, such as squares and rectangles, can be bent and deformed by forces – the sides can be moved and the angles between them altered.

However, by adding another beam across the middle of a square, you turn it into two triangles. The sides cannot be moved without breaking the beam, making the shape stronger and able to support more weight.

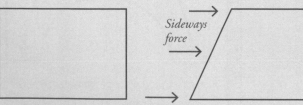

Sideways force

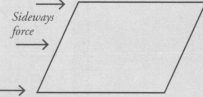

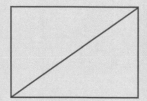

A rectangle has angles of 90° at each corner.

A sideways force will push the rectangle and change its shape.

Adding a diagonal beam between two corners turns the rectangle into two triangles, making it much stronger.

DOMES FROM ARCHES

A dome acts like an arch. Just as arches are a strong shape, so are domes. Domed roofs are common in mosques and have been used for hundreds of years. Around 500 years ago, a new cathedral in Florence, Italy, was given the largest dome ever built (it remained the largest until recently). The architects held a competition to come up with a way of building the planned dome without supports called buttresses. The contest was won by Filippo Brunelleschi, who made a wooden framework and then a skin of bricks on the inside and outside. He arranged the bricks so that stresses were passed sideways to the wooden struts. Any other arrangement would have allowed the force to act downwards, encouraging the bricks to fall on the people below.

Brunelleschi's dome in Florence uses forces to keep the bricks of the cathedral's dome in place.

see for yourself

Use straws or thick card stock to make different shapes, then test them by putting pressure on them. Which shapes are the most difficult to distort?

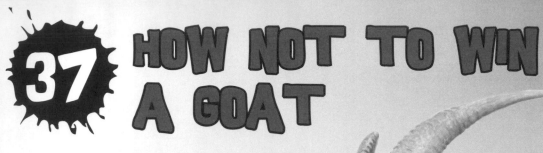

37 HOW NOT TO WIN A GOAT

Mathematics can help you to win games – even games that appear to be just a matter of chance. Chance is not as random as we like to think it is – you can sometimes improve your chances, even in a games that seem to depend on luck.

DO YOU WANT A GOAT?

About 50 years ago, there was a TV programme in the USA called *Let's Make a Deal*. The show was fronted by a presenter named Monty Hall, who gave his name to a conundrum (a type of puzzle) called the Monty Hall problem.

Imagine a TV show in which you could win either a car or a goat. Unless you really like goats, you would probably rather win the car.

Goats are very nice, but some people would rather have a car.

MILLIONS OF GOATS

The Monty Hall problem is slightly easier to grasp if you think of a game with a million doors and 999,999 goats. The chances of you picking the right door the first time are 1 in 1,000,000. The host opens 999,998 doors. There is a very good chance that the goat is behind the other door as your chance of picking the right door the first time was so small.

There are three doors on the stage. Behind one door is a new car, and behind each of the other doors is a goat – so there are two goats and one car.

Assume the goats stay completely quiet so that you cannot tell which doors they are behind. The presenter asks you to choose a door, which you do.

THE RIGHT CHOICE?

The presenter doesn't open the door you chose. He opens one of the other doors, showing that there is a goat behind it (he knows where the goats are). He then asks if you want to change your mind and switch doors. Should you change doors or stick with your first choice? Does it make any difference? Although it seems that it should not make a difference, by switching, you actually improve your chance of winning the car.

When you first chose a door, you had a 1-in-3 chance of picking the car. After the presenter opened one of the doors, there were two doors left, one with a goat and one with a car. The odds have changed… Suppose you picked Door 1. The table below shows the possible results. It's easy to see that if you switch door, you have a 2-in-3 chance of getting a car. If you stay with the same door, you have only a 1-in-3 chance of getting a car. Of course, if you would rather have a goat, you should not switch.

THE THREE PRISONERS

The Monty Hall problem is of no life-or-death importance, it just determines whether you need to build a garage or a goat-shed. The 'three prisoners' problem is rather more important.

Three prisoners are awaiting punishment. They hear that one has been chosen to be pardoned, but the others will die. The prison guard knows who will die and who will be set free. One prisoner begs the guard to tell him which of the other two will be executed. He says knowing will not make any difference because his fate has

Door 1	Door 2	Door 3	Result if switching	Result if staying
Car	Goat	Goat	Goat	Car
Goat	Car	Goat	Car	Goat
Goat	Goat	Car	Car	Goat

already been decided – but he thinks it will improve his chances of being the one who is pardoned. Is he right?

In fact, the prisoner's chances are not improved by knowing which other prisoner will die, but the chances of the other prisoner will improve! If our prisoner is prisoner A, he has a 1-in-3 chance of being freed. If he hears that prisoner B will be killed, his chance does not change. But prisoner C's chance of being saved increases to 2 in 3. Prisoner A cannot change his chances (as he could in the Monty Hall problem) because he does not have the option of swapping places with the other prisoner.

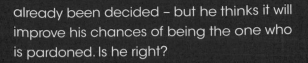

see for yourself

Instead of a car and some goats, you can use beads under cups. You will need two red beads, a blue bead and three identical cups. Remember where the beads are so that you can reveal one of the red ones when a friend picks a cup. Write down how many times your friend wins when switching. You need to test your friend at least 20 times to get a result you can trust.

38 HOW TO MAKE AN INFINITE PATTERN

Some patterns are simple; they repeat over a simple interval. Others are much more complicated and repeat themselves in smaller and smaller versions that can go on for ever.

COAST TO COAST

How would you measure the coastline of a country? If you followed it in an aeroplane, measuring how far you flew, you would get a measurement for the length. But it would not be the same as the figure you would get if you measured it all on your hands and knees with a tape measure. The coastline goes in and out in

Real snowflakes are fractals, and one of the easiest fractals to draw is the Koch snowflake. Begin by drawing an equilateral triangle (one with all sides the same length and all angles 60°). Now draw another equilateral triangle over the top of it, the other way up, to make a star, like the one in the middle. Each point of the star is an equilateral triangle in its own right. Do the same again, drawing a smaller equilateral triangle, upside down, over

each point of the star, so that it looks like the figure on the right. You can carry on dividing the outline in the same way for ever.

big sweeps, small bays and coves, and even smaller inlets and bumps – until you get right down to odd rocks and even stones. A pattern that is complicated and goes on and on at ever smaller levels is called a fractal. A coastline is not a perfect fractal as the smaller pattern is not an exact copy of the larger pattern – but it is the same in principle.

FRACTALS

A fractal is a pattern that copies itself exactly so that if you look at its details, you find they are copies of the larger pattern. There are many examples of fractals in nature. For example, when frost crystals form on glass, they make a spiky, branching pattern. If you look at the crystals through a magnifying glass, you will see that the individual branches also have tiny spiked branches coming off them, and those have even smaller branches, too. Lightning bolts have fractal forked shapes; cauliflower and broccoli flowers are made up of tinier versions of themselves; tree roots become ever thinner versions of the same shapes, as do blood vessels.

Ferns have leaves that are divided into smaller copies of the same shape. These leaves are called fronds.

Pythagoras tree

A Pythagoras tree is a fractal pattern that is easy to draw. Start with a square, then add two smaller squares balanced on their corners on top – and then two smaller squares on those, and so on. You could go on for ever, but you'd need to draw very small!

A LONG, LONG LINE

The Koch snowflake (like the one you drew on page 141) is a closed shape. It has a finite (restricted) area – but with an infinite outline, because the outline grows longer at every stage and there is no limit to the stages you can add.

As you add more and more triangles, the area continues to grow, but it grows more and more slowly. If we drew a graph of the growth of the snowflake, it would be an exponential curve (see page 181). But instead of going towards infinity, it would go towards zero instead. The change in the area comes closer and closer to zero, but it will never get there because you can keep adding triangles. This means that the area will keep increasing, even though by just a tiny bit.

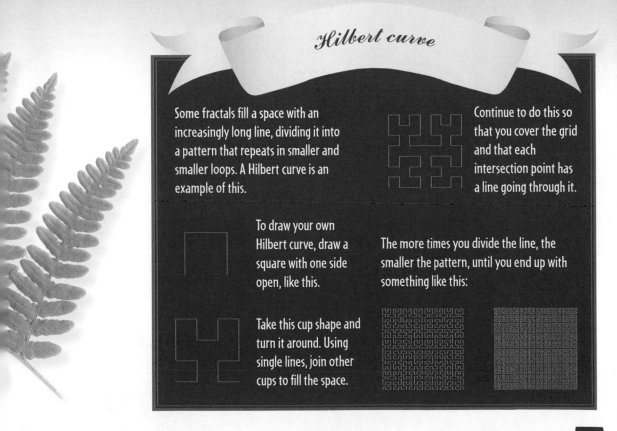

Hilbert curve

Some fractals fill a space with an increasingly long line, dividing it into a pattern that repeats in smaller and smaller loops. A Hilbert curve is an example of this.

Continue to do this so that you cover the grid and that each intersection point has a line going through it.

To draw your own Hilbert curve, draw a square with one side open, like this.

Take this cup shape and turn it around. Using single lines, join other cups to fill the space.

The more times you divide the line, the smaller the pattern, until you end up with something like this:

39 HOW TO BEND A BUILDING

There are many buildings that appear to be curved, but bricks are rectangular. So how do architects make curved buildings and roofs from straight edges?

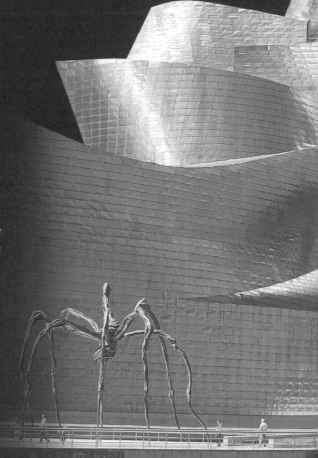

MORE ARCHES

Arched bridges have a curved opening, but if you look carefully at an arched bridge made of brick, you will see that the bricks are normal, rectangular bricks. A stone bridge may have stones that are wider at one end than the other, but they still have four straight sides. The bricks or stones are arranged so that the narrowest end is used to make up the inner curve of the archway. The same principle can be used to make whole curved buildings.

HOW ROUND IS A CIRCLE?

It's easy to arrange small bricks so that a wall or arch looks from a distance as though it is curved. Up close, you can see that the bricks have straight edges, but when you stand farther away, your eye does not see all the tiny straight edges. Instead, it blends them into a curve or circle. You can think of a circle as a shape made up of an infinite number of infinitely short lines, so a 'curve' made of small, straight bricks is similar to this.

The Guggenheim Museum in Bilbao, Spain, is a very curvy building.

LOOKING AT ANGLES

A standard brick is about 20 cm (8 in) long. The smallest closed shape you could lay out with bricks is a triangle with sides of 20 cm (8 in). There would be big gaps at the corners on the outside. You could make a square with four bricks, and an octagon with eight bricks. The gap to fill in at the corners would get smaller as you added more sides (more bricks) to the shape.

A full circle is 360°. The outside angle of each corner for a shape made from eight bricks would be 360 ÷ 8 = 45°. If you used 360 bricks you could make a shape with 360 sides and an angle of only 1° at each corner.

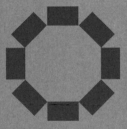

How wide will a circle of 360 standard bricks be? It has a circumference (boundary) of:
360 x 20 cm = 7,200 cm.

Using circumference = pi x diameter (see pages 104–7) you can work out that the width of the circle will be:
7,200 ÷ 3.142 = 2,292 cm, or 22.92 m.

STUPA-ENDOUS!

Building a curved wall is one thing – and people have done it for centuries. But building something curved in more than one direction is rather harder. One of the oldest and largest domed brick buildings is the Jetavanaramaya stupa in Sri Lanka, made 1,700 years ago. It's 122 m (400 ft) high and made from more than 93 million bricks. A stupa is a mound-shaped building for holding holy relics.

GHERKINS AND BALLS

Many modern curved buildings, such as the 'Gherkin' in London, UK, are made of plates of flat glass held in a network of steel struts. Flat surfaces are arranged to make the illusion of a surface that is curved in three dimensions. If you look at a football, you can see how this works.

Putting curves to use

Most curved buildings have curves so that they look good, but making curves from flat panels has practical uses, too. The solar tower at Odeillo in France is made with mirrors arranged in a curve. The curve reflects the rays of the Sun onto a single place. The Sun's rays carry heat as well as light, and the Odeillo furnace uses the heat from the rays to heat a furnace used for melting iron. There are 63 flat mirrors making up the surface that looks curved.

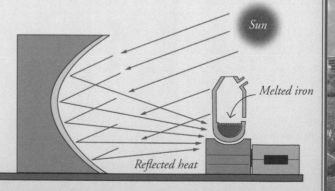

Sun

Melted iron

Reflected heat

A football is stitched together from hexagons and pentagons. It has a total of 32 faces (20 hexagons and 12 pentagons). The ball's shape is made by cutting off all the corners from an icosahedron, which is a shape with 20 triangular faces.

 The domes of the Eden Project are made of small hexagonal panels.

The pentagons are essential – only a flat surface can be made from hexagons, which is why hexagons can be used to tile a flat floor or wall, but pentagons allow the shape to curve and close into a ball.

A similar shape, using hexagons, is used in the domes of the Eden Project in Cornwall, UK. This uses thin plastic panels between a steel framework, and is inflated, so that the surface is actually curved because the panels are a little bendy.

see for yourself

Draw a square on a piece of paper; use a ruler so that the edges are straight and the same length. Now measure and make marks to divide each side into thirds. Draw a line between the two points on either side of each corner so that you have an octagon (eight-sided shape). Do the same thing again, and the shape will have 16 sides. Do it again. See how the shape becomes closer and closer to a circle?

40 HOW TO HAVE LESS THAN NOTHING

It is useful to be able to count your things – but how useful can it be to count things you haven't got? Negative numbers give us a way of counting what isn't there. You may wonder why you would want to...

COUNTING SHEEP

Human beings first began to keep tallies – using marks to show the number of certain objects – when they started to farm animals. The oldest mathematical records we have are tally sticks with marks apparently counting herds or flocks. Counting – giving a number rather than just a mark – developed from tallying.

One way of tallying sheep or goats is to keep a pile of stones – one stone for each animal. As each animal files past, move a stone to a new pile. At the end, if all is well, all the stones will have been moved and all the animals will be in the right place. If there are stones left over

when the animals have filed past, the remaining stones represent any missing animals. In a way, a stone in the wrong pile is equal to –1 sheep. It's telling you to go and look for the lost sheep.

YOU OWE ME

Trade became possible when people started counting instead of just tallying. And with trade comes the possibility of debt. Imagine you are a peasant who exchanges eggs for apples. Usually, you swap four eggs for four apples with a neighbour who grows apples but has no hens. Today, though, your hens are lazy and you have just two eggs.

Luckily, your neighbour agrees to give you four apples on the condition that you give him two extra eggs later. So now you owe him two eggs. In effect, you have –2 eggs. Getting two eggs (and passing them on) will return you to the position of having no eggs and no debt. We now use much more sophisticated methods of trading, but the principle is the same. If you borrow next week's pocket money to pay for something you want now, you have negative money until next week.

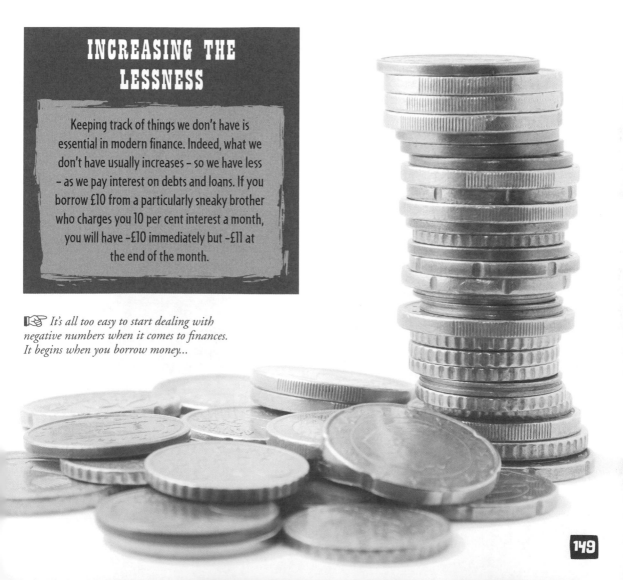

INCREASING THE LESSNESS

Keeping track of things we don't have is essential in modern finance. Indeed, what we don't have usually increases – so we have less – as we pay interest on debts and loans. If you borrow £10 from a particularly sneaky brother who charges you 10 per cent interest a month, you will have –£10 immediately but –£11 at the end of the month.

☞ *It's all too easy to start dealing with negative numbers when it comes to finances. It begins when you borrow money...*

149

LESS THAN ZERO

Some measurements can never go below zero – your hair can't be less than zero length, for instance. But whenever a scale has a chosen starting point – such as 0°C (32°F) on the temperature scale – it's possible for measurements to go into negative numbers. A really cold winter night in Siberia might be –50°C (–58°F). And the coldest temperature ever recorded on Earth was –89°C (–128°F) in Antarctica in 1983.

Another example of a scale that can go below zero is land height above sea level. Land that is –10 m (–33 ft) above sea level is actually 10 m (33 ft) below sea level and likely to flood.

HOW LOW CAN YOU GO?

Scientists sometimes use another scale for measuring temperature. Instead of using Celsius (°C) or Fahrenheit (°F), they use a scale called Kelvin. The zero of the Kelvin scale is called absolute zero and is at –273.14°C (–459.65°F).

☞ *At 0°C (32°F), water freezes into snow and ice, which is great for snowboarders. At lower temperatures, gases such as oxygen become liquids and they can even freeze if they get really cold.*

It really isn't possible for any temperature to be lower than absolute zero because all of the molecules that make up matter stop moving at that point. So far, nobody has found a temperature that low anywhere in the Universe.

ALL CHANGE?

When you run, you start off going quite fast, pick up speed as you warm up, and slow down as you get tired. When you go faster you are accelerating – the rate of change in your speed increases. As you slow down, you decelerate and the rate of change goes in the other direction – it's negative. Negative numbers are useful for measuring rate of change. If we didn't have them, you could only go faster and never slow down! (Of course, you could actually slow down, but we would have no way of describing it in mathematics.)

see for yourself

Look around your house for places where negative numbers or a minus sign are used. Your freezer will be set to a negative temperature. A TV remote control that alters the volume will have a minus button.

Backwards and forwards

Imagine a robot controlled by instructions. To make it go forwards, you give it a number and it moves forward that number of squares. How would you make it go backwards? Give it a negative number. It will have to subtract that number of squares from its current position and it does that by going backwards.

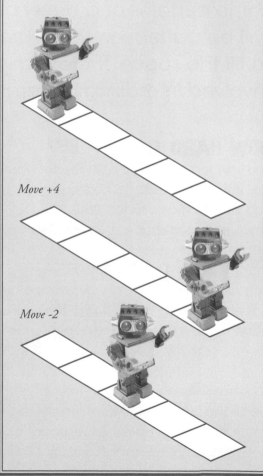

Move +4

Move -2

41 HOW TO TILE A PALACE

Do you have wallpaper in your bedroom? Or perhaps some curtains or a duvet cover? The chances are, there will be pattern on them. The pattern must repeat sensibly to fill the space. There is a lot of skill and mathematics involved in making patterns fit spaces.

HOW HARD CAN IT BE?

The simplest patterns that fill spaces easily are stripes, and patterns based around squares, such as a tartan. Patterns with small, repeated shapes, such as dots, are also regular and easy to work with. But many wallpapers and fabrics have more complicated patterns. When a decorator papers a wall, he or she has to line up the pattern at the edges of the paper so that it works properly.

A pattern has a 'repeat' – an interval at which the same elements of the pattern return. In the best patterns, the repeat is not obvious, so the pattern does not look like a lot of blocks of similar pictures.

The repeat can also be worked into the pattern so that we find the repetition satisfying. Where edges have to be matched, as they do when hanging wallpaper, a large repeat often means there is a lot of waste. The decorator has to cut off bits of the paper so that the next strip can start in the right place on the pattern.

☞ *Islamic architecture and art often uses very complex and beautiful patterns made from tiles.*

ON THE TILES

Wallpaper can be cut to different shapes, but it is usually used in long rectangular sheets. It is easy to fit rectangles together, even if you have to line up a printed pattern. Another way of covering a surface is by using tiles. Some tiles are just boring old squares and there is nothing hard about fitting them together. But some tiles use more complicated shapes.

GET MORE SHAPES!

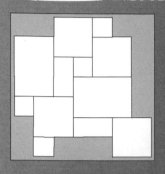

Some tiling patterns get around the problem of the limit on shapes that fit together by cheating – they use tiles of more than one shape. Some use variations on the same shape, such as squares and rectangles of different sizes.

Others use completely different shapes so that one shape can fill the gaps between the others. This pattern uses triangles and squares. There are lots of ways of colouring the squares and triangles to make different patterns from the same basic arrangement of shapes.

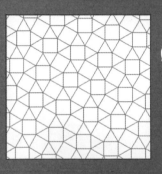

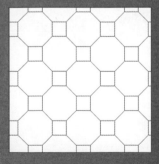

You can also use a mixture of eight-sided octagons and squares to fill a space.

FITTING SHAPES

Some shapes can be fitted together perfectly leaving no gaps. Equilateral triangles fit together, as do squares and hexagons. You can see hexagons fitted together in nature. Bees make honeycombs from hexagonal cells, for example. Circles cannot be used to fill a space exactly – there will always be gaps between the circles. Octagons cannot cover a space without leaving gaps, either.

In this pattern, the artist Escher has squares at the bottom that are slowly turning into tessellated lizards.

see for yourself

Copy one of the arrangements of tiles on the previous page and shade it in in different ways to make different patterns. Or see if you can make a tessellated picture like the Escher image. It's easiest if you start with a shape that will tessellate and then make a picture that fits the shape.

TESSELLATIONS

Shapes that fit together with no gaps are said to 'tessellate'. It's not just ordinary, regular shapes that can tessellate. Some of the cleverest patterns use rather odd shapes. Tiling patterns tend to use solid colours for the tiles to make up patterns, but there are cleverer ways of using tessellations. The artist M C Escher made many pictures from tessellated shapes. Sometimes he used the same shape and filled it in differently, and sometimes he used different shapes that fitted together perfectly. He used shapes that he turned into animals and people. Some of his patterns even had shapes slowly changing into other shapes, or evolving, as the pattern went across the page.

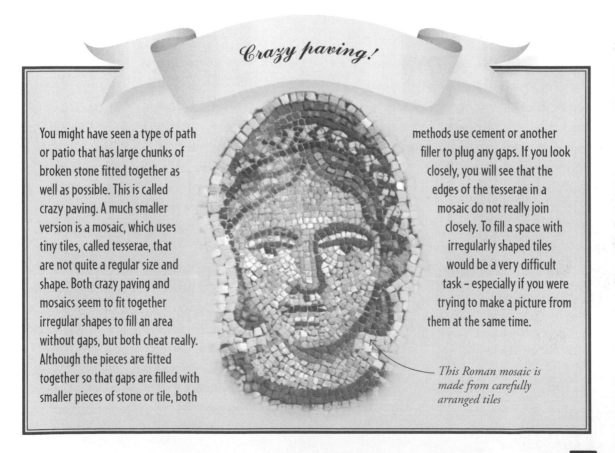

Crazy paving!

You might have seen a type of path or patio that has large chunks of broken stone fitted together as well as possible. This is called crazy paving. A much smaller version is a mosaic, which uses tiny tiles, called tesserae, that are not quite a regular size and shape. Both crazy paving and mosaics seem to fit together irregular shapes to fill an area without gaps, but both cheat really. Although the pieces are fitted together so that gaps are filled with smaller pieces of stone or tile, both methods use cement or another filler to plug any gaps. If you look closely, you will see that the edges of the tesserae in a mosaic do not really join closely. To fill a space with irregularly shaped tiles would be a very difficult task – especially if you were trying to make a picture from them at the same time.

This Roman mosaic is made from carefully arranged tiles

42 HOW TO WIN THE LOTTERY

It would be great if you could win a fortune and not have to worry about getting a job after school. But what are the chances?

A TOSS OF A COIN

If you a toss a coin, there is a 1-in-2 chance of it coming down heads and a 1-in-2 chance of it being tails. But what would happen if you tossed the coin more than once?

 *The potential results increase rapidly with each toss of the coin.*

With one toss, there are two possible results, so the chances of each are 1-in-2 (1:2), or 50 per cent. With two tosses, there are four possible combinations: the first can be heads or tails, and for either of these the second can be heads or tails (see the diagrams on the next page).

The chances of getting any combination on this second round of tosses are 1-in-4 (1:4) or 25 per cent. With three tosses, there are eight possible results. So with two possibilities (heads or tails), the number of possible results for the sequence doubles each time we toss the coin again.

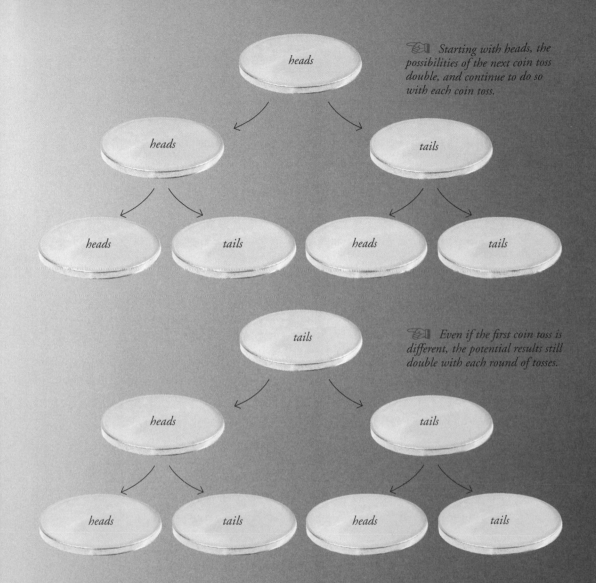

heads

heads tails

heads tails heads tails

👉 *Starting with heads, the possibilities of the next coin toss double, and continue to do so with each coin toss.*

tails

heads tails

heads tails heads tails

👉 *Even if the first coin toss is different, the potential results still double with each round of tosses.*

ROLL OF THE DICE

If you roll a die, there's a 1-in-6 chance of getting a three, a 1-in-6 chance of getting a two, and so on. If you toss two dice, each has a 1-in-6 chance of getting a three, but the chance of them both getting a three is 1 in 6 x 6 = 36. If you had three dice, the chances of them all coming up three would be 1 in 6 x 6 x 6 = 216.

ALL IN ORDER

If you roll two dice, there is only a 1-in-36 chance of getting two 3s, but there are two ways to get 3 and 4, so there is a 1-in-18 chance of that (2 in 36). If you are interested in the total score from the dice, the chances get more complicated – there's only one way to get 12, so the chance is 1 in 36, but you could get a 7 in six ways (6 and 1; 1 and 6; 2 and 5; 5 and 2; 3 and 4; 4 and 3), so the chance is 1 in 6 (6 in 36).

PLAYING FOR HIGH STAKES

With a game such as a national lottery, the chances of a win are very small – and that's why the prize is usually big enough to change your life.

Suppose a national lottery is played with six balls, and each ball has a number from 1 to 50 on it. If you pick a single number, and pull out a single ball, the chance of the ball matching your number is 1 in 50. If you pulled out two balls, the chance of one matching your number would be 2 in 50. Now, suppose you have chosen two numbers and pull out two balls; the chance of both your numbers being chosen is 1 in 50 for the first and 1 in 49 for the second ball (assuming the first ball is not returned).

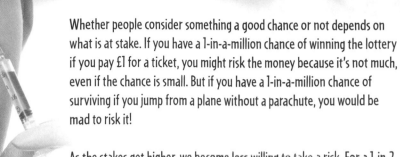

Whether people consider something a good chance or not depends on what is at stake. If you have a 1-in-a-million chance of winning the lottery if you pay £1 for a ticket, you might risk the money because it's not much, even if the chance is small. But if you have a 1-in-a-million chance of surviving if you jump from a plane without a parachute, you would be mad to risk it!

As the stakes get higher, we become less willing to take a risk. For a 1-in-2 chance of winning a large prize, we might buy quite an expensive ticket, but if a new medical treatment had a 1-in-2 chance of making your illness worse, you might well refuse it. Vaccination programmes rely on people taking the tiny risk of a side effect from the injection rather than the risk of serious illness if they are not vaccinated.

So the chance of getting both is 1 in (50 x 49), or 1 in 2,450. As the national lottery has six balls, the chances of getting all six balls correct is 1 in (50 x 49 x 48 x 47 x 46 x 45), or 1 in 11,441,304,000 – that's more than 1 in 11 billion!

With up to 50 numbers to choose from, the chances of winning the lottery are tiny!

see for yourself

Imagine you are playing a game in which you have to guess four numbers between 1 and 100 before they are flashed up at random on a screen. What are the chances that you will get all four numbers? (Each number can be flashed up only once.)

Answer:
The chance is 1 in 100 x 99 x 98 x 97
= 1 in 94,109,400

43 HOW TO EXPLAIN ANYTHING

Do ice cream sales go up if the temperature rises? And if they do, can we say one causes the other? How do we know whether hot weather causes people to buy ice cream, or whether buying ice cream causes the temperature to rise?

CAUSE AND EFFECT

Newspapers and TV reports often use statistics (numbers and graphs) to show a link between two or more events or trends and to try to explain one thing in terms of another. But can you trust them?

You have probably seen graphs that show how carbon dioxide in the air has increased, such as the one below. These are often put with graphs showing how the temperature of the world has increased over the same period.

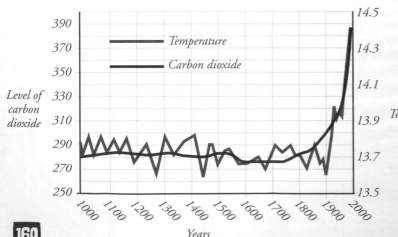

☞ Graphs such as this one show increases in temperature and levels of carbon dioxide – but which increased first?

The graphs show that higher levels of carbon dioxide and hotter temperatures go together. This relationship is called a positive correlation.

WHICH CAME FIRST?

On its own, the graph does not show which of the two comes first. We can't tell whether extra carbon dioxide causes the world to get hotter, or whether the rising temperature leads to more carbon dioxide. We need more information to work this out.

Burning fossil fuels, such as coal and oil, produces carbon dioxide, and this changes the atmosphere so that the world becomes hotter. Knowing the science, we can explain the relationship (correlation) shown by the graph, but we could not work it out from just the graph.

GETTING THE WRONG END OF THE STICK

It's easy to put two sets of numbers or graphs together and suggest that there is a relationship between them, and many people will believe it. People who think children watch too much TV or play too many computer games sometimes point out that children are heavier than they used to be, or read less, or take less exercise, and say that this shows that playing computer games and watching TV is harming children. It does not show it at all – there may be a link, or there may not.

As temperatures rise, ice sheets melt and the polar bears that live on the ice sheets can be stranded.

HOT AND BOTHERED

Mathematicians calculate the degree of correlation between two factors to decide whether there is a real relationship between them or not and what it is.

Suppose sales of ice cream go up as the temperature rises. They might compare the rates of rise – do ice-cream sales go up steadily at the same rate as temperature? They might look for key points – do ice-cream sales peak at a particular temperature?

This might mean that all of the people who like ice cream are already buying it. They may look at whether sales stay high if the weather stays hot. If they do not, perhaps people get fed up with ice cream, or can't afford to keep buying it.

Knowing all of this information helps ice-cream sellers to predict how much ice cream they will sell as things get warmer.

Changes in temperature can affect a lot of things, including sales of ice cream, swimming outfits and air-conditioning units.

THERE'S MORE TO IT THAN THAT

Suppose someone noticed that at the same time as sales of ice cream rose in a seaside town, so did drowning accidents. They might jump to the conclusion that eating ice cream made people more likely to drown. But just because both figures rise, doesn't mean that they are directly linked.

There is often another factor that people have ignored or not thought of. If the weather is hot, people buy more ice cream. They are also more likely to go boating or swimming. If more people are swimming and boating, more of them might drown. So there is no link with ice cream, but both the ice-cream sales and the rate of drowning go up as the weather gets hotter.

Backwards and forwards

It's easy to think that there is a link between things if you can see a pattern. The number of pirates has decreased as the temperature of the world has increased. Does that mean that global warming kills pirates, or that a lack of pirates causes global warming? Neither – it's just a coincidence.

see for yourself

Do you think there is a link in each of the following cases? What is the link likely to be?

The number of cows in South America has increased while the number of jaguars has decreased.

In 1910, lots of people bought anti-comet pills and anti-comet umbrellas to protect them from being killed by Halley's Comet. Nobody was killed by the comet.

Answers:
There is a link: Jaguars live in the forest; the forest has been cut down to make farms where cows are kept. Cutting down the forest has driven away the jaguars.

There is no link: the comet was never going to kill anyone and the pills and umbrellas had no effect.

44 HOW TO KNOW WHAT EVERYONE THINKS

Have you ever read news stories about surveys and thought to yourself, 'But they didn't ask me'? Surveys usually ask only some people their views, not everyone. Whether the information collected is useful and true, depends on the mathematics behind the survey.

QUESTION TIME

The way a survey is carried out affects the accuracy of its results. If you wanted to know how many people go to the cinema and you stood outside the cinema to ask people, your results would not be very accurate because many of the people you asked would be on their way to the cinema. You would get a very different result if you asked people outside a supermarket, or if you asked people at home.

If you wanted to find out which type of film people liked, you could ask them at the cinema because then you would be choosing people who are interested in films, and they are the relevant population for your survey. The sample (the group of people you ask) should represent the people the investigation is about.

FROM THEM TO US

Usually, the results of a survey are extended to cover a larger population. This means that the trends discovered in the survey are assumed to apply to a larger group of people. The answers from the sample are counted and turned into percentages. So if you asked 100 people if they would use a new ice rink and 35 said yes, you could suggest that 35 per cent of people would use it.

WHAT DID YOU SAY?

The answers you get from a survey depend quite a lot on the questions you ask. To get reliable results, the choice, order and wording of the questions should not favour one answer over another. If you ask 'Do you think Dan is a bad leader?' You are encouraging people to say he is. An unbiased question would be: 'How do you rate Dan as a leader?' Good/Bad, Yes/No questions and tick-boxes for different options are good. These are called closed questions – people can pick only one of the answers you offer. If you let people write down their own answers, it can be very difficult to compare them. These are often open questions, as people can say anything. It's much easier to count answers, work out percentages, spot trends and draw graphs if you use closed questions with fixed answers.

☞ *There's no point in only asking people who go to the cinema, whether or not they go to the cinema – they would all say yes!*

Most countries carry out a census every now and then. This is a questionnaire that everyone has to answer. Governments use census data to keep track of how many people live in the country, who they are and what they are like. It helps them to plan things such as how many schools will be needed and where to build new hospitals. This is very different from the type of survey where the results from a small sample are extended to others, as everyone in the country has to fill in the form – the sample is the whole population.

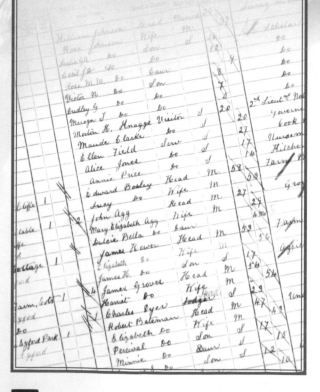

FIGURE IT OUT

Sometimes it is more effective to convert the percentages from a survey into figures. If you wanted the ice rink to be built, you might not want to say to your local council: '35 per cent want the rink,' because they could respond by saying: 'But 65 per cent do not want it.'

If there were 50,000 people in your town, it sounds better to say 17,500 people want the ice rink – this figure represents 35 per cent of 50,000. This sounds like a lot of people and may be enough to make it worth building an ice rink!

see for yourself

Carry out a survey among your friends and extend the results to the number of people in your class. Then ask everyone in your class the same questions. How accurate was your survey in telling you what people in your class think?

HOW MANY OF THEM?

The number of people involved in a survey is very important. If you want to extend the results to the whole population of a country, then you will need to ask a lot of people. On the other hand, a quick question to just a couple of your friends will not give you a reliable answer. The size of the sample – the number of people you ask – must relate to the total number of people you *could* ask.

So if the total population is 50 million, then asking five is no good, but a sample of 5,000 might be good enough. If the population is 250, asking 25 is acceptable if it is a straight Yes/No question.

CHOOSE ME!

You have probably seen questionnaires in magazines or on pieces of paper that are handed out in town centres. It might seem as though these are a fair way of collecting information, but often the view they give is not typical of the whole population.

The sample is made up of the people who choose to fill in questionnaires – this is called a self-selecting group, because they volunteer to answer the questions. More people of one type or view than another might be the ones who fill in the questionnaires and this could affect the results of the survey.

167

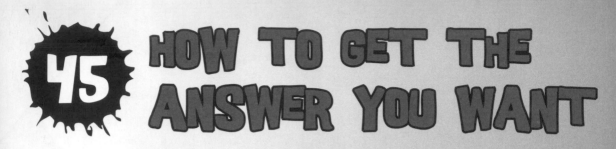

45 HOW TO GET THE ANSWER YOU WANT

Do you know how to get your parents to give you the answer you want by asking a question in the right way? It is easy to get what you want if you know how to use numbers and psychology.

MAKE THEM FEEL BAD

Most people don't like to be different from others. This means that you can use statistics in your favour. If you say: '80 per cent of the children in my class are allowed to...' that makes your parents look strict if they don't let you do the same. And if you say: 'Most reasonable people agree...' that makes it very hard for anyone to disagree!

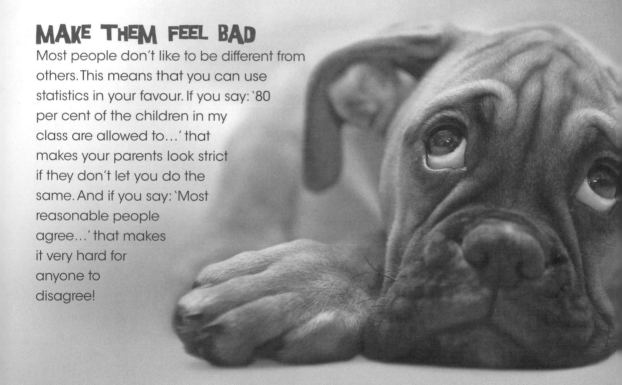

MAKE NUMBERS WORK FOR YOU

Numbers can always be presented in more than one way. You have probably seen adverts that say things like: 'It costs you just 50p a day to insure your phone… that is less than a litre of milk.' By concentrating on the small sum each day, they make the price sound modest. If you translate it into £15 a month, or £180 a year, you soon realize that it adds up to a sum you could use for more than milk. It may be enough to buy a new phone!

People campaigning for change might say: 'Nearly half of the residents want…' Although this means more than half don't want the change, we are swayed by seeing the word 'half' and we are therefore likely to agree.

If more than half of the people want it – even if it's only one more than half – they can say 'Most people want…' and again we are likely to agree.

Dogs have a habit of making you feel bad to get what they want - it's something we've learnt to do, too.

IT'S ALL IN THE MIND

You don't need to use numbers at all. If you wanted to go to the park, which question should you ask?

'I don't suppose I could go to the park, could I?'

'Can I go to the park, please? I'll be back in time for tea.'

You should use the second. The first question invites an answer of 'no' because it shows you are expecting it. The second answers the objection your parents may come up with before they have time to make it, and saying when you will be back assumes that you will be allowed to go.

You can also seem to offer choices, but only offer the answers you will accept. For example, 'Do you want me to come home at six or can I stay later?' does not make it easy for someone to say 'you can't go at all' – it just looks unreasonable!

46 HOW TO COUNT THE ATOMS IN THE UNIVERSE

You already know there is no end to counting – we can just carry on adding numbers for ever. But when we have very big numbers, we need new ways of talking about them. This does not stop them being mind-boggling, but it does help us to judge just how boggled our minds should be!

NOT SO BIG

We are used to hearing numbers in the millions and billions. These are often used to talk about people, money or website hits: India has a population of a billion, an online video may have a million hits. But what about bigger numbers? People often use made-up number names to mean just 'lots and lots' – gazillion and squillion are examples. There are real names for numbers that go up quite a long way. A centillion, for example, has 303 zeroes!

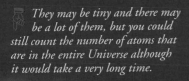
They may be tiny and there may be a lot of them, but you could still count the number of atoms that are in the entire Universe although it would take a very long time.

WHAT USE ARE THEY?

What could you count with those very big numbers? We will have to take over other planets before we can count human populations in anything larger than billions, but there are other things to count:

The first planet photographed outside the Solar System is about five quadrillion kilometres away.

A one-sextillion pengo banknote was produced in Hungary in 1946 (not for a very rich person, but because the currency was worth very little).

There may be ten sextillion stars in the Universe.
Earth weighs about six octillion kilograms.

The number of bacteria on the planet may be around a nonillion.

1,000,000 million (6 zeroes)
1,000,000,000 billion (9 zeroes)
1,000,000,000,000 trillion (12 zeroes)
1,000,000,000,000,000 quadrillion (15 zeroes)
1,000,000,000,000,000,000 quintillion (18 zeroes)
1,000,000,000,000,000,000,000 sextillion (21 zeroes)
1,000,000,000,000,000,000,000,000 septillion (24 zeroes)
1,000,000,000,000,000,000,000,000,000 octillion (27 zeroes)
1,000,000,000,000,000,000,000,000,000,000 nonillion (30 zeroes)

WHAT'S IN A NAME?

It is difficult to use number-names such as septillion, because most people do not know immediately how many zeroes there are and so how big the number is. It gets worse – different countries use different words for the same numbers, and even use the same words for different numbers. Instead of struggling with this, we can use international scientific notation. This sounds complicated, but it only involves counting the number of zeroes (or other digits) in a number.

☞ *Even if you counted all the grains of sand in this sand castle, you wouldn't get close to a googol!*

THE POWER OF TEN

Any number can be shown as a power of ten. The raised number after the ten shows the power to raise it to. This means you multiply ten by itself that many times. Because to multiply by ten we just add a zero, it also represents the number of zeroes the number has. So:

$10^1 = 10$
$10^2 = 100$
$10^3 = 1,000$
...
$10^{10} = 10,000,000,000$

Silly names for silly numbers

The name of the number 10^{100}, which is 1 followed by 100 zeroes, is a 'googol'. The name was invented in 1938 by Milton Sirotta, the nine-year-old nephew of the mathematician Edward Kasner. And there is a name for 10^{googol}; it's a googolplex. But this number is larger than anything that could ever be counted. Indeed, the number of subatomic particles in the Universe is about 2.5×10^{89}, which is not even a googol!

WHAT, NO ZEROES?

Not all numbers start with one and are followed by a bunch of zeroes. For more complicated numbers, we show them as a number between one and nine, multiplied by a power of ten. So:

$$5,000,000 = 5 \times 10^6$$

and

$$327 = 3.27 \times 10^2$$

Increasing the power of ten by one makes a huge difference.

IS THIS THE BIGGEST NUMBER THERE IS?

The biggest number that has ever been named is called Graham's number. It is so large, there is no way of writing it using any of the normal methods. If all the matter in the Universe was turned into a pen and a lot of ink, there wouldn't be enough to write down the number. Oddly, the mathematician who came up with the number, R L Graham, was struggling with a particular problem – and other mathematicians think the answer to the problem might actually be six.

see for yourself

Try writing out a googol (1 followed by 100 zeroes) using a stopwatch to time how long it takes. Now imagine how long it would take you to write out a googolplex. Remember that it's going to be 10^{100} times as long. Don't work it out, just have a guess.

Answer:
It probably took you around 40 seconds to write out a googol, but that gives you no idea of how long it would take to write a googolplex! It would take much longer than all the time that has passed since the start of the Universe, more than 13 billion years ago.

47 HOW TO MAKE A GHOST

You may have heard people say something odd-looking was a 'trick of the light' – and light can be very tricky. We can use the way light behaves and a bit of mathematical knowledge to make our own tricks using the power of light.

PEPPER'S GHOST

Stage ghosts that can mysteriously appear and disappear in the middle of the stage are an impressive trick to pull off in a crowded theatre. Today, we have computers to make special effects, but in the past when a ghost was needed on stage it was all done with mirrors, making something called 'Pepper's Ghost'.

USING MIRRORS

To make the ghost, a large sheet of plate glass was set at an angle to the floor (for a below-stage ghost) or the backdrop (for a ghost in the sides, or wings). The person playing the ghost was hidden out of view of the stage in a darkened room, with a mirror set up to bounce his or her reflection onto the plate glass. When the ghost needed to appear, a strong light was switched on in the ghost room, and the ghost's reflection bounced onto the glass to appear on stage. The ghost could move, too! The actor just moved around the hidden ghost-room. It could also disappear instantly when the light was turned off.

With the help of large mirrors and powerful lights, ghosts can appear on stage and disappear just as quickly. They might be a little more scary than this one, though!

ANGLES AND ANGELS

Angle of incidence   *Angle of reflection*

When a beam of light hits a mirror, it bounces off – but there is a pattern to the way it bounces. The reflection bounces off the mirror at the same angle as the light beam strikes the mirror. Mathematically speaking, the angle of reflection is the same as the angle of incidence. Imagine a line at right-angles to the mirror, coming out of the mirror and into the room. A beam of light striking the mirror at 30° to the right of this line will be reflected 30° to the left of it. And, of course, a beam of light coming from the left will be bounced off at the same angle to the right. This explains why a mirror image reverses the real world.

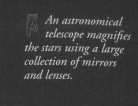
An astronomical telescope magnifies the stars using a large collection of mirrors and lenses.

Up and around

You can make your own periscope using a long rectangular box, such as a juice carton, and two small mirrors like the ones sold to carry in a handbag. Cut holes at opposite ends of the box, on opposite sides. Fix the mirrors to the inside of the box at an angle of 45° above the top hole facing downwards, and below the bottom hole facing upwards. The mirrors will bounce a reflection of the outside world (from the top hole) to your eye (looking into the bottom hole).

You don't need to go in the sea to test your periscope. You can use it to see over walls, or turn it sideways and use it to look around corners in your house or school instead.

UP, PERISCOPE!

Reflections can be used for more useful things than creating ghosts. Microscopes and telescopes both work by bouncing light around using curved lenses that magnify the image. Submarines use periscopes with carefully arranged mirrors to let their crew see what is happening on the surface of the sea while the submarine lies hidden under the waves.

A periscope is an L-shaped tube with mirrors on the inside. The mirrors bounce a reflection of the outside world around the corner in the tube and down to the observer. Periscopes can also have magnifying lenses to make them work as a telescope at the same time.

PLAYING WITH LIGHT

If you have ever used a kaleidoscope, you have played with mirrors to make a changing pattern. A kaleidoscope uses a small number of chips made from coloured plastic or glass and an arrangement of mirrors to build up a symmetrical pattern.

A kaleidoscope is a long tube, with a small hole at one end that you look through. The other end has a transparent cover, usually plastic or glass, that lets in light. At the light end, there is a chamber to contain the coloured chips. If you make your own kaleidoscope, you can use any items, including sequins, paperclips and glitter, in the chamber. By shaking or rotating this chamber, you create different patterns and shapes.

In the main part of the kaleidoscope's tube, the mirrors are arranged in a triangle, with the mirrored sides facing inwards towards each other. This is the bit that does the work. Light from the coloured shapes hits the mirrors. It is bounced from one mirror to another mirror to produce a pattern of reflections that you can see by looking through the eye-hole. As you shake or turn the kaleidoscope, the things in the chamber move and the pattern changes. Although the arrangement of the coloured glass or plastic is random, the repeated reflections make a symmetrical pattern. Some kaleidoscopes do not have any shakable objects. Instead, they just reflect and break up the view of the world at the end of the kaleidoscope.

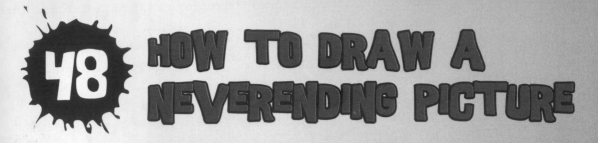

48 HOW TO DRAW A NEVERENDING PICTURE

An old toy, called an Etch A Sketch, lets you draw lines on a screen by twiddling buttons. It is impossible to leave a break in the lines, so you have to work out how to make a picture by drawing a continuous line – it's an interesting problem!

THINK OUTSIDE THE ENVELOPE

It's easy to do a drawing if you can start and end the lines wherever you like. It is much harder if you can't lift your pencil from the paper and are not allowed to go over a line you have already drawn.

See if you can work out how to draw this open envelope without lifting the pencil from the page:

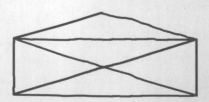

Puzzles like this make you think about pathways and routes, and see line segments and sequences. To draw this envelope without lifting your pen, you will need to think very carefully about where to start and which route to take.

CROSSING BRIDGES

The German mathematician Leonhard Euler came up with a problem based on a map of the city Königsberg. The city is built on a group of islands. The question was whether it was possible to walk

Amazingly, this picture of the Taj Mahal in India was drawn on an Etch A Sketch using a continuous line.

through the city crossing every bridge once – and only once. He eventually proved that there was no such route through the city.

Euler realized that where the bridges were did not matter, neither did the route taken within any island. But what did matter was the way the bridges related to each other.

Each island is called a node, and each bridge is a line. To solve the, problem all that matters is how many lines (or edges) join each node. Euler decided that for a person's walk to cross each line once, there must be either no nodes with an odd number of lines, or just two nodes with an odd number of lines.

49 HOW TO HAVE A MILLION BROTHERS

Don't underestimate the power of two. Two may seem like a small number, but doubling things gets you to very large numbers really quickly!

ALL THE RICE IN THE WORLD

There's an old Indian story in which Lord Krishna appears in disguise to a king and challenges him to a game of chess. If he wins, Krishna says, he wants a prize of some grains of rice. Krishna does win, and demands grains of rice counted out in this way: a single grain of rice on the first square of the chessboard, two grains on the second square, four grains on the third square, and so on. The king thinks it a measly prize, but soon the squares cannot hold the grains of rice. Halfway across the board, the king owes Krishna more than four billion grains of rice.

The rice for square 35 would weigh around 1,000,000 kg (2,200,000 lb), or as much as ten blue whales. On the 64th square, the king would need more than 9,223,372,036,854,7750,808 grains – enough to cover the whole of India with rice to a depth of 1 m (3 ft).

BROTHERS AND SISTERS

Everyone has (or had) two parents, four grandparents, eight great-grandparents, and so on, the number doubling with each generation. That's fairly obvious. But what happens as you go further back? You need only to look back 31 generations – around 750 years – to find that you have more ancestors than the whole population of the planet. And that means everyone has the same ancestors so we are all related to each other!

A REALLY BAD BUG PROBLEM

Aphids, or greenfly, are tiny insects that cover plants and suck the sap from them, sometimes killing them. Aphids have a neat trick to help them multiply very quickly. For much of the year, they clone themselves – so they don't need to look for a mate, and young aphids have only one parent. An aphid can begin cloning itself after five days, and produces up to ten clones a day. So after ten days, there are the original aphid and 50 clones, which will soon start cloning at the rate of ten a day each. By the end of a month, if no aphids die, there will be nearly a million. This pattern of rapidly growing numbers is called exponential growth.

Populations can grow exponentially, the rate of growth becoming faster and faster

Population

Time

50 HOW TO MAKE MONEY FOR NOTHING

If you have lots of money, you can put it in a box and hide it in your room, or you can put it in the bank. By putting it in the bank you can get money for nothing. The bank also gets money by lending your cash to someone else.

JUST A LITTLE...

Most people need to borrow money at some point. Even if they can pay for most things, they don't usually have enough to buy a house or a car without borrowing. When people borrow money from a bank, the bank charges them a little bit extra, called interest. Imagine a bank called the Mathematical Bank. It prides itself on using round numbers for all its business so that things are easy to follow. A woman wants to borrow £1,000 from the bank to pay for a holiday.

The bank lends her the money at a rate of 10 per cent interest per year. This means that if she borrowed the money for a whole year, she would owe the original £1,000 and an extra 10 per cent at the end of the year. As each per cent is one hundredth of the amount, 10 per cent is £100, so she would owe £1,100.

... AND A LITTLE MORE

Suppose the woman kept the money for another year without paying any of it back. (The bank would not usually allow this, but as it's the Mathematical Bank it's special.) At the end of the second year, she would owe £1,100 plus another 10 per cent of that, which is another £110 – a total of £1,210. And at the end of the third year, she would owe £1,210 plus 10 per cent, so £1,210 + £121 = £1,331. The bank has made £331 just from passing time.

The interest builds up as time passes, with interest being charged on the interest. This is called compound interest, and it can very quickly get out of hand. Look at how the woman's debt could build up if she didn't pay any of it back:

	Start of year	Interest at 10%	End of year
Year 1	£1,000.00	£100.00	£1,100.00
Year 2	£1,100.00	£110.00	£1,210.00
Year 3	£1,210.00	£121.00	£1,331.00
Year 4	£1,331.00	£133.10	£1,464.10
Year 5	£1,464.10	£146.41	£1,610.51
Year 6	£1,610.51	£161.05	£1,771.56
Year 7	£1,771.56	£177.16	£1,948.72
Year 8	£1,948.72	£194.87	£2,143.59
Year 9	£2,143.59	£214.36	£2,357.95
Year 10	£2,357.95	£235.79	£2,593.74

LOOKS SMALLER, BUT ISN'T

Some lenders try to make it look as though they are not charging much interest by giving a monthly figure instead of a yearly figure. But 1 per cent compound interest on £1,000 each month for 10 months is not the same as 10 per cent of £1,000 in one go. By the end of 10 months at 1 per cent, the debt has grown to £1,104.62, which is more than the £1,100 it would have been after a year at 10 per cent. After 12 months, the debt at 1 per cent per month would be £1,126.83.

GIVING WITH ONE HAND, TAKING WITH THE OTHER

The bank lends money – but where does the money come from? The bank borrows money from people who have more than they need, or who want to save. It attracts savers by offering them interest on their savings – so the bank pays people a little more than they pay in, in just the same way as it charges people a little more than they borrow. The bank does not pay as much interest as it charges, though, so it always makes money.

The Mathematical Bank charges 10 per cent on loans, but pays out only 5 per cent on savings. So to lend the woman £1,000 for her holiday, it pays a saver 5 per cent of £1,000, which is £50. It collects £100 back, so it makes £50 on the deal.

Most people take out insurance to protect against losing something valuable. If you have a nice bike, you might insure it so that you get money for a new one if it is stolen. Lots of people buy insurance, but not many bikes are stolen, so the insurance company makes money.

Suppose 50 people each pay £10 to insure a bike worth £100. The insurance company collects 50 x £10 = £500. If only two bikes are stolen, it has to pay out only £200. Insurers use very complex mathematics to make sure they assess the risks properly and hardly ever lose out.

see for yourself

Collect some leaflets offering loans and savings deals. How much would you have to pay back after a year if you borrowed some money? How much would you get if you saved the same amount?

GLOSSARY

AXIS
One of the lines that show values on a graph.

BACTERIA
A very tiny living organism that can be seen only by using a microscope. Some bacteria cause disease.

BILLION
1 followed by 9 zeroes.

CIRCUMFERENCE
The outline of a circle.

CONSECUTIVE
Something that is in order, with no gaps in the sequence. For example, 4, 5 and 6 are consecutive numbers.

COORDINATES
The numbers that define a precise point on a graph or map.

DATA
Raw information (often numbers) that has not been processed to give results.

DATA POINT
A single point on a graph.

DENSITY
How much a particular volume of a material weighs. You can work out the density by dividing the mass of a material or object by its volume.

DIAMETER
A straight line passing through the centre of a shape such as a circle or sphere.

DIGIT
A single number. For example, 1 and 2 are both digits.

DILEMMA
A problem that is really difficult to solve because none of the possible solutions seem acceptable.

DNA
Short for deoxyribonucleic acid, DNA is the very complex chemical that carries the genetic code of living things. Only identical twins have the same DNA.

ENCRYPT

To turn something into a code to keep its information secret.

EXPONENTIAL CURVE

A line graph that starts with a small slope but becomes steeper and steeper very quickly, showing an ever-increasing rate of change.

FINITE

Describes something that has an end or a limit.

FREQUENCY

The number of sound waves per second.

HEXAGON

A shape with six sides.

INFINITE

Describes something that continues for ever without end.

MOLECULE

The smallest indivisible particle of a chemical substance.

PENTAGON

A shape with five sides.

PITCH

How high or low a sound is.

POLYGON

A closed shape with any number of straight sides.

PROPORTION

A share or portion of something, related to the size of the whole.

QUINTILLION

1 followed by 18 zeroes.

RANDOM

Describes something that does not follow any order or pattern.

RATIO

A relationship between two quantities, shown using a colon (:). For example, if a map has a scale of 1:50,000, 1 cm on the map is equal to 50,000 cm or 500 m on the ground.

SEPTILLION

1 followed by 24 zeroes.

TRILLION

1 followed by 12 zeroes.

Quercus Publishing Plc
21 Bloomsbury Square
London
WC1A 2NS

First published in 2011
Copyright © 2011 Quercus Publishing plc

Created for Quercus by Tall Tree Books Ltd
Text by Anne Rooney
Index by Susie Brooks

UK and associated territories: ISBN 978 0 85738 602 1
US and associated territories: ISBN 978 1 84866 148 6

Printed and bound in China

10 9 8 7 6 5 4 3 2 1

Picture credits
4 and 96-97 Innovari/Dreamstime.com, 5 and 22-23 © Dmitry Kalinovsky/Dreamstime.com, 6 and 72-73 inno4ka200/Dreamstime.com, 6 and 151r Claudio Fichera/Dreamstime.com, 7 and 62-63 Wikicommons/Cybershot800i, 7b and 118-119 Pniesen/Dreamstime.com, 9b Nataliya Evmenenko/Dreamstime.com, 10l Shutterstock/Georgy Markov, 12 Dreamstime.com 14l © Saša Prudkov/Dreamstime.com, 15br Dreamstime.com, 17m Kirsty Pargeter/Dreamstime.com, 19 Panctonvideo/Dreamstime.com, 19r Wlikicommons/Josell7, 24-25 Maxpro/Dreamstime.com, 26-27 NASA, 28-29 Bowie15/Dreamstime.com, 32-33 Eraxion/Dreamstime.com, 34-35 Tmts/Dreamstime.com, 36-37 Jgroup/Dreamstime.com, 38 Jgroup/Dreamstime.com, 40-41 Farek/Dreamstime.com, 42-43 Angelo Giampiccolo/Dreamstime.com, 43r Charlie Hutton/Dreamstime.com, 45r Yegor Tsyba/Istock, 47r NASA, 49r Norman Chan/Dreamstime.com, 50-51 Wikicommons/Walther, 52 Redbaron/Dreamstime.com, 55 Wikicommons, 56bl Slateriverproduction/Dreamstime.com, 58-59 Cammeraydave/Dreamstime.com, 59br Hudakore/Dreamstime.com, 61l 2008 Getty Images, 64tr Vladimir Kindrachov/Dreamstime.com, 65 Wikicommons/Howcheng, 66 Ayvan/Dreamstime.com, 67 Wikicommons, 68-69 Billyfoto/Dreamstime.com, 70tr sgame/Shutterstock, 73tr Wikicommons, 75 tracy lorna/Istock, 76-77 Alesnowak/Dreamstime.com, 78-79 Jodielee/Dreamstime.com, 79br Aprescindere/Dreamstime.com, 80-81 Jgroup/Dreamstime.com, 82-83b xavier gallego morel/Shutterstock, 83br Coinman62/Wikicommons, 84bl Tomboy2290/Dreamstime.com, 85br NASA/Wikicommons, 86b Mdf/Wikicommons, 87b Dreamstime.com, 89l Philip Lange/Shutterstock, 90-91t Feferoni/Dreamstime.com, 91b Andrew tk tang/Wikicommons, 92-93 Franckito/Dreamstime.com, 93br Roberto197/Dreamstime.com, 94-95 Jlye/Dreamstime.com, 97bl Wikicommons, 98b Idreamphoto/Dreamstime.com, 100-101 Prometeus/Dreamstime.com, 102l Sandralise/Dreamstime.com, 103c Charles Minard/Wikicommons, 105-106 Kelpfish/Dreamstime.com, 106br Amilevin/Dreamstime.com, 107t Joze Pojbic/Istock, 108-109 Rtimages/Dreamstime.com, 110-111 Puma330/Dreamstime.com, 112-113 Rambleon/Dreamstime.com, 114-115 NASA, 116-117 Brancaleone/Dreamstime.com, 116b Italianestro/Dreamstime.com, 117ar Tom Dowd/Dreamstime.com, 120-121 Johan63/Dreamstime.com, 122tl Carolinasm/Dreamstime.com, 124-125 Carlart/Dreamstime.com, 127tr Viorel_dud/Dreamstime.com, 128-129 Virynz/Dreamstime.com, 129br Wikimol/Wikicommons, 130-131 Flynt/Dreamstime.com, 132-133 Pics1/Dreamstime.com, 135r Doctorjool/Dreamstime.com, 136-137 Marionrodd/Dreamstime.com, 139r Ljupco/Dreamstime.com, 140-142 Stelogic/Dreamstime.com, 143 Birdboy/Dreamstime.com, 144-145 Matthi/Dreamstime.com, 146-147 John R Smith/Shutterstock, 150-151 Konstantin Shishkin/Dreamstime.com, 152-153 Galyna Andrushko/Shutterstock, 154l Zaqarbal/Wikicommons, 155b Neilnell/Dreamstime.com, 156 Jgroup/Dreamstime.com, 157 Wikicommons, 158tr Sapientisa/Dreamstime.com, 158brPeterfacto/Dreamstime.com, 159r Showface/Dreamstime.com, 161 Freezingpt/Dreamstime.com, 162 Chuck Schmidt/Istock, 165 Deklofena/Dreamstime.com, 166-167t Nikanovak/Dreamstime.com, 168-169 Apeyron/Dreamstime.com, 170-171 Ilex/istock, 172-173b Alesnowak/Dreamstime.com, 174-175 Reinhold68/Dreamstime.com, 176 Evgenly_p/Dreamstime.com, 178-179 Wikicommons, 180-181 Sharpshot/Dreamstime.com, 180-181 Feng Yu/Dreamstime.com, 182c Py2000/Dreamstime.com, 184-185 Ironrodart/Dreamstime.com